Cooking Under Pressure

Also by Lorna Sass

Whole Grains for Busy People

Whole Grains Every Day, Every Way

Pressure Perfect

The New Vegan Cookbook

The Pressured Cook: Over 75 One-Pot Meals in Minutes

The New Soy Cookbook

Short-Cut Vegan
(formerly titled *Lorna Sass' Short-Cut Vegetarian*)

Great Vegetarian Cooking Under Pressure

Lorna Sass' Complete Vegetarian Kitchen
(formerly titled *Recipes from an Ecological Kitchen*)

Cooking Under Pressure

In Search of the Perfect Meal

A Collection of the Best Food Writings of Roy Andries de Groot
(Selected and Edited)

Christmas Feasts from History

Dinner with Tom Jones

To the Queen's Taste: Elizabethan Feasts and Recipes

To the King's Taste: Richard II's Book of Feasts and Recipes

Cooking UNDER Pressure

Lorna Sass

wm

WILLIAM MORROW

An Imprint of HarperCollins*Publishers*

HarperCollins books may be purchased for educational, business, or sales promotional use. For information please write: Special Markets Department, HarperCollins Publishers, 10 East 53rd Street, New York, NY 10022.

FIRST EDITION

Library of Congress Cataloging-in-Publication Data

Sass, Lorna
    Cooking under pressure / Lorna Sass. —Twentieth anniversary ed.
        p. cm.
    Includes index.
    ISBN 978-0-06-170787-2
    1. Pressure cookery. I. Title.
    TX840.P7S36 2009
    641.5'87—dc22   2008045690

09 10 11 12 13 WBC/RRD 10 9 8 7 6 5 4 3 2 1

This book is dedicated to all those who want to eat better and faster—with the wish that time saved in food preparation will be spent relaxing around the dinner table with family and friends.

The Twentieth Anniversary Edition is dedicated to those who want to slash cooking time, save fuel, and conserve all of our planet's precious resources.

Contents

Acknowledgments

I would like to express my gratitude to my mother, who went to India and brought back a pressure cooker instead of a sari. Without her particular set of priorities, this book might never have been born.

I am also grateful to my dear friends who endured months of hearing my voice on an answering machine while I was "under pressure" developing recipes. Many of these same friends (plus some new ones) became charter members of the Pressure Cooker Elves Club, an organization originally established to retest the recipes in this book and now composed of ardent converts to the pleasures of pressure cookery. They include: Pat Baird, Judy Bloom, Ann Brady, Joyce Curwin, Marilyn Einhorn, Suzanne Hamlin, Dana Jacobi, Bill Kelly, Rose Keough, Bob and Bridget Lyons, Charmian Reading, Steve Schmidt, and Rebecca Wood. Hearty thanks to you all!

And special thanks to:

Ann Bramson, senior editor at William Morrow, for recognizing the value of this project long before the pressure began to build, and for her enthusiasm over the past year.

Laurie Orseck, project editor at William Morrow, for being so responsive to my requests, and for revising under pressure with such grace.

Helene Berinsky, for creating a book design that reflects the fun, excitement, and contemporaneity of pressure cooking.

Pat Baird, Bev Bennett, and Steve Schmidt for reading and commenting on the completed manuscript.

Bobby Troka, neighbor and friend, for providing a second home for a very spunky Burmese kitten who understood nothing about deadlines.

Richard Esposito for designing the type of kitchen that inspires creativity, and for holding my hand throughout a typically painful renovation.

Phyllis Wender, my agent, for taking the book contract with her on vacation.

Paula Wolfert, Suzanne Hamlin, Mayburn Kass, and Ceri Hadda for paving the way with their articulate enthusiasm for pressure cookery.

All of the pressure cooker manufacturers—Aeternum, BRA, Chantal, Cuisinart, Hawkins Futura, Kuhn-Rikon, Mirro, Presto, and T-Fal—who shared their time, knowledge, and cookware so generously.*

For this Twentieth Anniversary Edition, I am deeply grateful to David Sweeney, who did so much to promote this book when it first appeared and championed its return to print. Thank you, Cassie Jones, for enthusiastically adopting "my baby" and for bringing a fresh eye to the manuscript. Thanks also to Nicole Martella for so efficiently fielding requests, and to the rest of the team at William Morrow Cookbooks, including Lisa Gallagher, Lynn Grady, Tavia Kowalchuk, Kim Lewis, and Paula Szafranski.

---

*Note for Twentieth Anniversary Edition: Although BRA, Chantal, Cuisinart, and T-Fal stovetop cookers are no longer available, other brands have joined the ranks, including Fissler, WMF, and Fagor for stovetop cookers and Cuisinart for electric models.

"There is a gadget on the market that permits a cook to scoff at time. It is a pressure cooker...."

—IRMA S. ROMBAUER, *The Joy of Cooking, 1946*

Preface to the
Twentieth Anniversary Edition

As this special twentieth anniversary edition of *Cooking Under Pressure* goes to press, Mrs. Rombauer's claim that the pressure cooker "allows the cook to scoff at time" is even more relevant than it was when she penned those words more than sixty years ago: Because this magical appliance cooks food so quickly, it helps us conserve fuel as well as time. Because the cooker does such a great job of tenderizing tough cuts of meat, it saves us money.

Over the past two decades, my enthusiasm for pressure cooking has not faded. In fact, as I've learned more and more about the advantages of cooking under pressure, I have come to believe even more firmly that there is no better way to prepare a hearty soup, a soulful stew, or a delectable risotto in a flash. And aren't such homemade dishes what we long for in this era of multitasking and eating on the run?

The original edition of *Cooking Under Pressure* was so successful that I saw no reason to make any significant alterations of content or tone. Rather, I focused on lowering the fat in the recipes—one or two tablespoons rather than the formerly popular three or four—and reducing the amount of liquid since the cookers now available require less to come up to pressure. I've also inserted some useful techniques acquired since 1989.

I am delighted that *Cooking Under Pressure* is once again available to those who have been pressure cooking for decades and to those about to discover its many delights for the first time.

It is with great pride and pleasure that I serve it forth.

—*LORNA SASS*
New York City

Introduction

When I told my father that I was writing a pressure cooker cookbook, he recalled that on the day I was brought home from the hospital, some relatives unexpectedly appeared to meet the new baby. It was right around dinner time, and the year was 1945.

He and my grandmother turned right to the trusty pressure cooker, knowing that they could produce a meal in minutes: first some lentil soup (10 minutes), followed by stewed chicken (9 minutes) and potatoes and green beans (4 minutes). Then individual custards pressure-steamed in ramekins (5 minutes) for dessert.

Clearly the pressure cooker—with its ability to produce a tasty and nutritious meal in 30 minutes or less—has always had a great deal to offer the time-conscious cook. So it seems particularly odd that by the late fifties, some 45 million pressure cookers were unaccountably stowed away in attics and forgotten.

Perhaps home cooks were lured away by the ease and seeming glamour of TV dinners and other convenience foods. Perhaps there was just one story too many about a careless cook who ended up with split peas on the kitchen ceiling.

In Europe, India, and North Africa—where great value has always been placed on the kind of hearty soups and succulent stews that nurture the soul—the pressure cooker has never suffered a dramatic decline, and it's not uncommon to see two or three different sizes being used simultaneously to prepare dinner. Indeed, many of the dozen or so brands now available in this country are manufactured abroad. With their striking, sleek new designs and multiple safety features, they look right at home in the contemporary American kitchen.

I began thinking about pressure cookers when my mother carted one home from India in 1987 and asked to borrow a cookbook on the subject. To my surprise, I couldn't find any in my vast library of old books, and when she went searching in bookstores, she couldn't find any current ones either.

My mother had always been a bit ahead of her time, so I wasn't all that surprised when a few months later I read the headline "Look What's Back: The Pressure Cooker" in the September 1987 issue of *Food & Wine*. The article sang the praises of pressure cookery and rated the top five readily available brands. "Pressure cookers have returned to the well-equipped kitchen," wrote equipment specialist Mardee Haidin Regan, "not as collectibles from decades gone by, but as a nutritionally sound, fast and efficient means of preparing food."

The *New York Times* agreed. "Pressure cookers are making a comeback," declared Marian Burros in her column, "Eating Well" (February 3, 1988). "There is no clear explanation of why they ever went out of fashion," she continued, "but now they are particularly appealing because they make it possible to cook many healthful foods like dried beans and peas in a very short time."

A health-oriented eater myself, I was sold on the idea. The result is the volume you are now holding. Anyone who is new to pressure cookery or hasn't done it in a long time is about to embark on a wonderful adventure. Like most adventurers, you may feel a bit anxious as you wait cautiously for the pressure to rise that first time. But with this book and the newly designed safety-first cookers now available, this adventure should be nothing but fun and good eating: fast food at its wholesome best.

And I guarantee you that the pressure cooker has a natural place in the contemporary kitchen, where cooking under pressure has become a way of life.

Happy cooking!

—LORNA SASS
New York City

If you'd like information on purchasing a pressure cooker, contact me at www.lornasass.com or mail your request to Cooking Under Pressure, P.O. Box 704, New York, NY 10024. Please enclose a self-addressed, stamped envelope.

A Pressure Cooker Primer

The pressure cooker is a snap to use, and you'll have the hang of it in no time flat. For those worriers among you, I might add that with the newly designed, safe-to-use cookers, you really can't do any injury to yourself or your loved ones.

So if you'd like to dig right into the recipes and learn by doing, you can skip this entire section. (I won't be insulted because I won't know.) Just glance at Before You Start (page 21), find out the following from your manufacturer's booklet, and off you go:

- How to lock the lid correctly in place
- How to know when high pressure has been reached
- How to reduce pressure and unlock the lid

If you don't understand any of the phrases used in the recipes, have a look at The Language of the Recipes (pages 16–19), and you'll be back on track in a minute.

WHY I'M CRAZY ABOUT THE PRESSURE COOKER

I like to cook, but I'm not the type to enjoy spending the afternoon stuffing chicken wings, making puff pastry, or creating some elaborate French sauce based on Escoffier.

I like food that isn't fussy, fatty, or flat. Give me robust flavors, fork-tender meat, and liberal doses of well-seasoned vegetables and grains. And give them to me quickly.

That's what the pressure cooker does, and that's why it has taken up permanent residence in my kitchen.

WHAT IT DOES WELL AND WHAT IT DOESN'T

If asked what pressure-cooked dishes I love best, I would be hard put to decide among soups, stews, and risotto. I'm a great fan of soups, and they emerge from the cooker after 15 minutes tasting as if they'd been affectionately hovered over for hours. The same may be said for stews, those forever-simmering concoctions that I'd all but forgotten until the pressure cooker came along.

Pressure cooking has brought other foods into my life that I previously had neither the time nor patience to prepare. It was special cause for celebration when I took a chance and discovered that a risotto with superb texture could be pressure-cooked in 4 minutes—no stirring! Now it's become standard hassle-free company fare and gets rave reviews every time.

Whole grains and beans are ready within half an hour, without presoaking. Pot roast and brisket are fork-tender in an hour, and 15 minutes is all the time you need to pressure-steam an old-fashioned bread pudding.

Despite the wintry appeal of these wonderful comfort foods, don't be fooled into thinking of the pressure cooker only in terms of hearty cooking. It is a great boon for preparing fresh vegetables any time of year, and turns out a delicate rice pilaf in 10 minutes.

What doesn't the pressure cooker do well? Aside from the obvious, like baking cookies and grilling lamb chops, I see no real reason to cook fish under pressure since it can be prepared so quickly and efficiently by other means. I've made three exceptions: In the recipes for fish broth, chowder, and seafood risotto, the cooker does an outstanding job. See if you agree.

HOW IT WORKS

Once the lid is locked into place, the liquid inside the pressure cooker is brought to a boil over high heat and produces steam. Since this steam is sealed inside the cooker, pressure builds and the internal temperature rises.

At sea level, the atmospheric pressure is 14.7 pounds per square inch and the boiling point is 212 degrees Fahrenheit. When the pressure in the cooker is increased to 15 pounds above normal sea-level pressure, the boiling point of water increases to 250 degrees Fahrenheit.

There are many advantages to cooking at this higher-than-standard boiling-point temperature. Perhaps the most dramatic one is that under high pressure foods cook in about one-third the usual time. In addition, the steam pressure softens the fibers in food, tenderizing even the toughest cuts of meat in a matter of minutes. The steam also forces the ingredients to mingle in such a dramatic way that pressure-cooked foods become quickly infused with intense flavor. As a result, many recipes require less salt.

When the food is done, the pressure can be released in one of two ways. You can allow it to drop naturally by turning off the heat and letting the pot sit undisturbed. This usually takes 3 to 7 minutes, but can take as long as 20 for a full pot of soup or stew.

When timing is critical, the pressure can be "quick-released" in less than a minute by placing the cooker under cold running water. Many of the new models offer the option of leaving the cooker on the stove and quick-releasing the pressure by moving a lever or pressing a button.

TOTALLY SAFE

Cookers based on the traditional design have a removable pressure regulator that sits on the vent pipe and rocks gently, emitting a *chug-chug* sound when the pressure is up. Newer appliances with a more contemporary look—often referred to as "second-generation cookers"—regulate pressure with stationary valves and use indicator rods to reveal when the pressure is up. They make little or no noise. I worked with both types while testing the recipes for this book and found all of them simple and entirely safe to use, eliminating the pitfalls that beset our mothers and grandmothers.

You can expect to find the following safety features in all of the pressure cookers available today:

- The lid *must be locked* securely in place in order for the pressure to rise.
- An expanding rubber gasket makes it impossible to unlock and remove the lid until all of the pressure inside the cooker has been released.
- An overpressure plug and/or back-up vents begin to release steam (thereby preventing the pressure from continuing to build) if you forget to turn down the heat after high pressure has been reached, or in the unlikely event that the vent becomes clogged with food.

WHAT TO LOOK FOR

In a well-stocked housewares department, you are likely to find as many as half a dozen different cookers to choose from. There is also an excellent Web site, *www.pressurecookerworld.com* (866-409-8466), which displays dozens of cookers available for purchase and carries replacement parts.

Here are some guidelines to help you make a selection:

SIZE: If it's your first cooker, choose the largest one you can conveniently store; don't buy anything smaller than a 6-quart (or 6 to 7-liter, if European). Since you can fill the cooker only halfway when preparing beans and grains, and three-quarters for other dishes, you will find anything smaller than 6 quarts too limiting. If you are planning to make broths, opt for an 8- or 10-quart model.

DESIGN: The new cookers are gorgeous! Go for the one that makes you happy to look at.

LID: Designs for locking lids in place vary considerably. Play with the different models to discover which you find most convenient.

PRESSURE RELEASE: In all cookers, pressure drops naturally when the heat is turned off and the pot is left to sit. When using traditionally designed cookers with removable regulators, pressure can be quick-released only by setting the pot under cold running water. This is actually much easier than it sounds.

Cookers with stationary valves offer a variety of alternative methods for quick-releasing pressure without removing the pot from the stove. While a stovetop quick release can be very convenient, be forewarned that this method releases a good deal of aromatic steam into the kitchen.

HANDLES: Two heat-resistant handles are extremely welcome when you are moving the cooker to the sink to release pressure under water. Not all cookers have a second handle and not all handles are heat resistant.

CONSTRUCTION: Some recipes call for sautéing ingredients before cooking under pressure. Heavy-bottomed stainless-steel cookers that are well constructed and conduct heat evenly are best for this function. In addition, a thick bottom with a copper or aluminum sandwich prevents scorching when you are bringing the cooker up to pressure over high heat. Avoid cookers with nonstick finishes; these tend to become scratched, thereby shortening the life span of the pot.

LIQUID MINIMUM: The less liquid required to bring up the pressure, the more versatile the cooker. (See How Much Liquid? page 10.)

Check the manufacturer's minimum requirements; amounts vary from ½ cup to 2 cups.

HOW MUCH LIQUID?

Because the lid is tightly sealed and relatively little steam escapes during cooking, recipes generally require less liquid than normal. (Of course, this does not hold true for soups.)

Vegetables can be braised in ½ to ¾ cup of liquid, while meats usually require around 1 cup to produce a nice amount of gravy. Dried fruits, beans, and grains must be made with more generous amounts of liquid because they absorb so much as they cook.

The liquid called for is often water, but may also be broth, tomato

---

Doing a "Wet Run"

Some cookers don't lose any liquid in the form of steam and others can lose as much as 3 cups! I have tested the recipes in cookers that lose less than ½ cup of liquid. It is wise to determine how much liquid your cooker loses so you can compensate, if necessary, by adding extra liquid at the beginning. For example, if you are making a pot roast that requires 1 hour under pressure and your cooker loses 2 cups of liquid during that time, to avoid scorching and have sufficient gravy, you will need to add 2 extra cups of water or broth to the amount called for in the recipe.

There is very little work involved in this "wet run," but you will need to be around the kitchen for 1 hour and use a timer. For a detailed explanation of the phrases used in these steps, see The Language of the Recipes (page 16).

1. Pour 4 cups of water into the cooker.
2. Lock the lid in place.
3. Over high heat bring to high pressure.

---

sauce, wine, or beer. Ingredients containing a good deal of water, such as cabbage, onions, and canned tomatoes, also figure into the minimum liquid requirement since they release so much liquid as the pot comes up to pressure. So, for example, if your cooker requires a 2-cup minimum to come up to pressure, a 14-ounce can of tomatoes (including juice) plus ¼ cup of water or broth is more than sufficient.

Milk, cream, and yogurt are best blended in after the pressure is released, as they have a tendency to curdle, scorch, and foam. Wine should be used with discretion since its flavor is intensified in pressure-cooked dishes.

Since cookers with rocking pressure regulators tend to release

4. Reduce the heat just enough to maintain high pressure and cook for 20 minutes.
5. Quick-release the pressure under cold running water.
6. Remove the lid, tilting it away from you to allow steam to escape.
7. Pour the water into a measuring cup and see how much water the cooker has lost in the 20 minutes under pressure.
8. Mark down the water loss below.
9. Return the water to the cooker.
10. Repeat steps 2 through 8 two more times and mark down the water loss below. Don't be tempted to assume that after 40 minutes your cooker will lose two times the water it lost after 20 minutes. It doesn't always work that way.

After 20 minutes, my cooker loses _____cups of water.
After 40 minutes, my cooker loses _____cups of water.
After 1 hour, my cooker loses _____cups of water.

more steam than those with stationary valves, they sometimes require slightly more liquid when preparing such "dry" dishes as rice or grain pilafs. It's a good idea to do what I call a "wet run" (see box, pages 10–11) to determine how much liquid your cooker actually loses.

To compensate for variations among ingredients and cookers, I often call for slightly more liquid than may be necessary. As you gain experience with your own cooker and with the recipes, you may want to reduce the amount of liquid somewhat, but always heed your manufacturer's recommendations about the minimum required. Keep in mind, too, that these recipes have been tested in a 6-quart cooker. If you are using a larger one, check your manual to see how much liquid is necessary to bring the contents up to high pressure.

TIMING MATTERS

Time is traditionally counted from the moment high pressure is reached, but for vegetables and other delicate foods, total cooking time provides a more accurate measurement (see page 17).

As a general rule, the more food and liquid there is in the cooker, the longer it will take to come up to high pressure. A full pot of soup or stew, for example, can take as long as 20 minutes. To save time when preparing large quantities, turn on the flame as soon as you put the liquid in the pot and bring it toward the boiling point as you prepare and add the other ingredients. Alternatively, add liquid that is boiling hot. Once you've locked on the lid, the pressure will come up in half the time. (Timing under pressure remains the same.)

In most recipes, I've given a range of time under pressure since timing varies among cookers. Start off using the shorter timing and if you find food consistently undercooked, move to the higher timing.

The shape and size of ingredients affect cooking time. When you combine vegetables, for example, those that cook quickly must be cut into larger pieces than those that cook slowly. For this reason, whenever the thickness of a sliced vegetable or a cube of meat is stipulated in the recipes, it should be taken seriously.

Unlike the microwave, the quantity of food in the cooker does not affect the length of cooking time once high pressure is reached—whether you cook one beet or ten beets, the amount of time it takes to cook them under high pressure remains the same.

COOKING ON AN ELECTRIC STOVE

Electric coils create intense heat and are slow to respond to adjustments in temperature. The adjustments you've learned to make for standard stovetop cooking carry over to pressure cooking, but there are a few special considerations:

**The cooker is traditionally brought up to pressure over high heat. If utilizing the highest setting causes scorching, try bringing up the pressure using a slightly lower setting. Alternatively, place a heat diffuser (see page 23) under the cooker before bringing it up to pressure.

**Once the cooker reaches high pressure, the heat must immediately be lowered or the pressure will continue to build. To accommodate to the coil's slow response, lower the heat a few minutes before high pressure is reached. Alternatively, transfer the cooker to a burner preset to low—or whatever you've determined to be the correct setting for maintaining high pressure.

**When the recipe calls for the natural pressure release, move the cooker to a cool burner.

COOKING OVER A HIGH BTU FLAME

To avoid scorching, bring up the pressure over medium heat—or whatever flame you consider equivalent to high on a standard gas range. Alternatively, place a heat diffuser (see page 22) under the cooker before bringing it up to pressure.

COOKING ON AN INDUCTION RANGE

Check with the manufacturer to be sure that the cooker will function properly. If so, place the cooker in the middle of a marked heat zone that is the same size or smaller than the base of the cooker. Follow the instructions for Cooking on an Electric Stove on the previous page.

USING AN ELECTRIC PRESSURE COOKER

Electric cookers are less versatile than stovetop models, but many people value the fact that they can be programmed to begin and end cooking and left completely unattended.

**Use the BROWN setting to do any cooking required before bringing up the pressure.

**Program the cooker for HIGH PRESSURE.

**If the recipe calls for Natural Pressure Release, reduce cooking time by 2 minutes to adjust for the longer time it takes for electric cookers to release the pressure naturally.

**If the recipe calls for quick-releasing the pressure by setting the cooker under cold running water, subtract 3 minutes from cooking time and allow the pressure to come down naturally for 3 minutes. Then press the quick-release button in very short spurts while averting your face from the steam. If any liquid is ejected from the valve, wait about 30 seconds before proceeding.

**Use the BROWN setting to do any final cooking after the pressure is released.

HIGH-ALTITUDE COOKING

The pressure cooker is a boon for those living at high altitudes, where the boiling point of water is lower and foods cook more slowly. To use these recipes at 2,000 feet and higher above sea level, increase cooking time by 10 percent and then in 10-percent increments until you discover the best formula for perfect cooking time at your altitude.

CLEANING AND MAINTAINING YOUR COOKER

Pressure cookers require a little more maintenance than the average pot. The pots themselves are usually dishwasher-safe, but the lids are not. Check your owner's manual for details.

REMOVING AND CLEANING THE GASKET: To preserve the life of the rubber gasket (sealing ring), remove it from the lid and rinse it after each use. Allow the gasket to air-dry thoroughly before setting it back in the lid. Although gaskets usually last for years, it's wise to have a backup on hand for the moment when it no longer creates a tight seal.

CLEANING THE VENT/VALVE AREAS: Whenever you wash the lid, examine these areas and, if necessary, scrub them free of debris with a soapy nonabrasive scouring pad or a toothbrush. If you own a jiggle-top cooker, you may need to poke a toothpick through the vents to be sure they are clear. If you use a second-generation cooker, you will occasionally need to unscrew the pressure regulator and wash the parts well. Look for detailed cleaning instructions in your owner's manual.

SCOURING THE BOTTOM: If the bottom is encrusted with scorched food, sprinkle in some nonabrasive cleanser such as Bon Ami. Add about 2 cups of water and bring to a boil. Let sit for a few hours or overnight. Scrub clean with a scouring pad.

If the bottom interior or exterior becomes stained, scrub it with a nonabrasive product called Bar Keepers Friend, available in some supermarkets and many houseware stores. To locate a source in your area, call 800-433-5818.

TIGHTENING THE HANDLES: If the handles become loose, tighten them with a screwdriver.

STORING: Rest the lid against the side of the cooker or set it upside down on top of the cooker. If the gasket isn't thoroughly dry, drape it loosely on the lid. Don't lock the lid in place for storage or you'll be greeted by a strong whiff of your last meal when you next open the cooker.

ACCESSORIES

One of the great joys of the pressure cooker is that your whole meal can be made in one pot and there is little more to clean than the tasting spoon.

But one small piece of equipment is critical to successful pressure cookery: a good timer. Many foods are not harmed by an extra minute or two of intense cooking, but some are positively ruined. Why take a chance? Use a timer and relax. I recommend a digital one that can be set for seconds as well as minutes.

Cookers come with either an aluminum rack or a trivet and a steaming/drainer basket for cooking foods (primarily vegetables and desserts) above the liquid. If yours doesn't have either, you can use a standard collapsible steaming rack.

In addition, for a handful of the recipes in this book, you'll need one of the following:

—a 5-cup heatproof soufflé dish (or suitable alternative that fits comfortably into a 6-quart cooker) for making bread puddings and custards
—individual 4-ounce (½-cup) heatproof ramekins for making custards, puddings, and timbales
—a 7- or 8-inch (depending upon the diameter of your cooker) springform pan for making cheesecakes. If you can't locate this size locally, a good mail-order source is Zabar's in New York City (*www.zabars.com*).

THE LANGUAGE OF THE RECIPES

A few phrases used in the recipes are particular to pressure cookery:

SET THE RACK IN PLACE: Place the rack on the bottom of the cooker. If your appliance doesn't come with a rack, use the trivet, or the trivet in conjunction with the steaming basket.

LOCK THE LID IN PLACE: Follow your manufacturer's instructions. If the lid is not locked properly, the pressure won't rise.

OVER HIGH HEAT, BRING TO HIGH PRESSURE: Depending upon the quantity and contents in the cooker, it will take anywhere from 30 seconds to 20 minutes to bring the pressure up to high. Apply maximum heat to reach high pressure as quickly as possible.

ADJUST THE HEAT TO MAINTAIN PRESSURE: Once high pressure is reached, reduce the heat to medium-low to maintain it; otherwise the pressure will continue to build, creating loud hissing noises. (Just remember not to reduce the heat too much, or the pressure will start to drop.) After using the cooker a few times, you'll have a better idea of the amount of heat required to maintain high pressure. If you have an electric stove, you may have to move the cooker to another burner for a minute since the coils are slower to respond than a gas flame.

UNDER HIGH PRESSURE: Your instruction manual will explain how to recognize when maximum (13 to 15 pounds) pressure has been reached. All recipes in this book have been tested under high pressure. Unless otherwise noted, cooking time begins from the moment that high pressure is reached.

For example, above each recipe is a phrase such as "3 minutes *under high pressure.*" This means that as soon as the cooker reaches high pressure, you should set the timer and cook under high pressure for 3 minutes.

TOTAL COOKING TIME: I use this term almost exclusively in the chapter on vegetables. Since delicate vegetables can be easily overcooked, set the timer from the moment the lid is locked into place. Above each of these recipes is a phrase such as "3 minutes *total cooking time.*" This means that you should release any pressure that has built in the cooker—*whether or not* high pressure has been reached—after 3 minutes have elapsed. Remove the lid immediately.

USE A QUICK-RELEASE METHOD: When the timer goes off, bring down the pressure by placing the cooker under cold running water, or use an alternative method suggested by your manufacturer. (If the alternative method produces any sputtering, stop engaging the release mechanism and bring the pressure down under cold running water instead.) Recipes for preparing such easily overcooked foods as chicken and vegetables *require* the quick-release method.

LET THE PRESSURE DROP NATURALLY: When the timer goes off, turn off the heat and let the pot sit until the pressure drops of its own accord; depending upon the quantity and contents in the pot, this can take from 3 to 20 minutes. The food continues to cook as the pressure drops.

With rice or cheesecake, the natural pressure release is required for successful results, and it's the only way to be sure of achieving tender beef. In these cases, after timing under high pressure is indicated, you will see a phrase like "then 7 minutes for natural pressure release." This means that the lid should be kept in place for as long as indicated, even if the pressure has already dropped.

In some recipes—for example, many soups and stews—you have the option of letting the pressure drop naturally or using the quick-release method. When time permits, I always let the pressure drop naturally. I can't prove it, but I'm convinced that taste and texture are better as a result.

REMOVE THE LID, TILTING IT AWAY FROM YOU TO ALLOW STEAM TO ESCAPE: Even when the pressure is completely released, there is residual steam in the pot so, for safety's sake, make it a practice to tilt the lid away from your face when removing it.

REPLACE THE LID AND COOK FOR A MINUTE OR TWO IN THE RESIDUAL HEAT: When delicate foods such as rice or fresh vegetables are only slightly underdone after the pressure is released, set (but don't lock) the lid in place and let the food cook in the heat that remains in the pot, without applying any additional heat.

FORBIDDEN FOODS

Many manufacturers warn against cooking foaming ingredients such as applesauce, cranberries, pearl barley, rhubarb, and split peas for fear that the foaming action will catapult a small bit of food into the vent and clog it. I've avoided cranberries, rhubarb, and plain split peas, but I *have* discovered methods for cooking applesauce, pearl barley, and pea soup that caused no problems in multiple testings. Just follow the recipes carefully, and keep an eye on the pressure gauge and vent when these ingredients are cooking.

Always reduce the pressure under cold running water when cooking foaming foods, and never attempt to force open the lid.

ADAPTING RECIPES

Pressure cooking bears a strong resemblance to many forms of stovetop cooking—namely boiling, steaming, and braising—so adapting your favorite recipes to the cooker is easy. Look for recipes in this book that resemble the ones you want to try in the cooker and substitute ingredients. For example, take your favorite lamb stew recipe and compare it with a few of the lamb stews in the meat chapter. Use the same amount and cut of lamb and the same quantity of liquid, but substitute the liquid, spices, and vegetables of your choice.

Check the list beginning on page 173 to see how the vegetables should be cut to cook properly in the time allotted. Remember, too, that you have the option of giving long-cooking ingredients a head start, then quick-releasing the pressure and adding ingredients that require shorter cooking times.

In some cookers, it is possible to regulate the pressure so that food can cook at low (5 pounds; 228 degrees Fahrenheit), medium (10 pounds; 238 degrees Fahrenheit), or high (15 pounds; 250 degrees Fahrenheit) pressure. A few manufacturers offer guidelines for cooking at different pressures. Because some cookers don't have this flexibility, all of the recipes in this book have been tested under high pressure—which has the added advantage of getting the food on the table that much more quickly.

Before You Start

COOKERS: Quantities in the recipes that follow are calculated for *6-quart cookers.* All of the recipes can be cooked in an 8-quart (or larger) cooker. If you're using the 4-quart model, make sure that the ingredients don't fill the cooker beyond the manufacturer's recommended maximum. If they do, either halve the recipe or cook it in two batches.

Unless otherwise noted, the recipes can be successfully prepared in any brand of cooker. The only exceptions are those cookers that require more than ¾ cup of liquid to come up to pressure; you'll find special instructions in these instances.

COOKING TIMES: I usually give a range of cooking times since timing can be only approximate at best, and doneness is often a matter of taste. To avoid overcooking, release pressure after the minimum recommended cooking time has elapsed. If the food is slightly undercooked for your taste, simmer it, covered, for a minute or two over medium heat. If considerably more cooking is required and there is still some liquid on the bottom of the pot, lock the lid back in place and bring the cooker back up to pressure, which takes only a minute or two.

Since timing is based on cooking over gas, owners of electric stoves may need to make minor adjustments. Always move the cooker to another burner before releasing the pressure.

BROWNING: A number of recipes call for browning meat or sauté-ing onions and garlic before adding liquid and other ingredients. To avoid scorching, scrape up any browned bits sticking to the bottom of the cooker before locking the lid in place and bringing up to pressure.

STICKING: Sometimes dishes with relatively little liquid, such as a thick split-pea soup, a grain pilaf, or a rice and bean stew, will stick to the bottom of the cooker and become crusty or burnt. If you carefully spoon out the food and leave behind the damaged layer, the flavor will not be affected; clean the pot after a brief soaking in water. Or you can eliminate the problem altogether by using a heat-diffusing device such as a "flame tamer" (available in housewares stores). First set the cooker directly on the heat to bring it up toward high pressure. Shortly before high pressure is reached, set the flame tamer under the cooker and continue cooking over high heat. As soon as high pressure is reached, reduce the heat to maintain high pressure and continue as directed in the recipe.

SOME HANDY TECHNIQUES

CLEANING AND CHOPPING LEEKS: Trim off the root end. Begin slicing from the root end upward, discarding bruised outer leaves as you go. Even the dark green inner leaves may be used since the cooker does a fine job of softening them. Swish the chopped leeks vigorously in several changes of water to release and discard all sand.

ZESTING LEMONS, LIMES, OR ORANGES: Use organic citrus, if possible. Wash the fruit thoroughly. The best tool for zesting is a rasp called a microplaner specifically designed for this purpose; it is available in many kitchen shops. You can also use a standard zester or the finest side of a box grater.

JUICING LIMES OR MAKING LIME WEDGES: To maximize the yield of juice, slice the lime lengthwise a little off center so that you avoid the core. Continue slicing wedges around the core. Squeeze the wedges to extract juice. Discard the core.

TOASTING NUTS AND SEEDS: Toast nuts on a baking pan in a toaster oven (most convenient) or standard oven set to 375 degrees until fragrant and lightly browned, 2 to 4 minutes in a toaster oven and slightly longer in a standard oven. Toast seeds in a skillet set over medium-high heat; stir them frequently. Nuts and seeds burn easily, so watch them closely.

ROASTING RED PEPPERS: Set each pepper on a grid raised above a gas burner and turn the heat to high. Rotate with tongs until thoroughly charred. (If using an electric oven, cut the peppers in half, remove the seeds, and core. Press firmly to flatten. Set cut side down under the broiler, as close to the broiling element as possible.) Wrap each charred pepper in a wet paper towel and enclose in a plastic bag to steam. When cool, use the paper towel to rub off the skin. Remove the core and seeds. If not using the peppers immediately, toss them in olive oil and refrigerate in a tightly sealed container for up to 5 days.

Broths and Soups

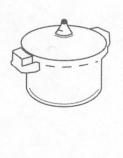

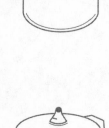

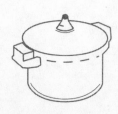

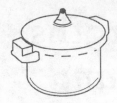
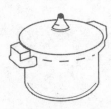

⬗ BROTHS ⬗

I t's a joy to make broths and soups in the pressure cooker. The ingredients quickly mingle, resulting in the full-flavored, long-simmered taste characteristic of good home cooking. Gratification can be almost instant, as the homemade soup is set on the table only moments after the idea of preparing it comes to mind.

Until I started using the pressure cooker, I was the type of cook who thought it quaint and honorable to make homemade broth, but I rarely seemed to get around to doing it. I would always feel a bit guilty as I threw away the chicken giblets or the leek greens and broccoli stalks, reaching yet again for a canned broth or instant bouillon.

The pressure cooker began changing all of that for me, as soon as I discovered that I could make a broth from scratch in the time it took me to stack the dishwasher and scrub the pots after my dinner guests left.

The broth recipes were tested in a 6-quart cooker. You can increase the ingredients by 50 percent if you own an 8-quart cooker, and double the ingredients for a 10-quart. Add only enough water to reach the maximum capacity level recommended by the manufacturer.

It is best to prepare meat broths a day in advance so that you can skim off the fat that congeals on top after overnight refrigeration. Put the solid ingredients in the steaming basket if your cooker comes with one; lift the basket out after cooking and voilà—you'll have a strained broth.

Allow about 20 minutes for a full pot to come up to high pressure—less if you add broth or water that's already been brought to a boil in a separate pot or teakettle.

Beef Broth

The pressure cooker produces a wonderfully rich and gelatinous broth in an hour, and the leftover stewing meat can be turned into a delicious hash. Browning the beef before adding the water contributes to a richer flavor, but I don't think it's worth the extra time and effort.

This broth can be refrigerated for 5 days and frozen for up to 4 months.

MAKES APPROXIMATELY 1½ QUARTS

(1 HOUR UNDER HIGH PRESSURE)

2½ pounds beef shins (shanks) or stewing beef cut into 1-inch cubes

1½ pounds beef bones

2 large carrots, cut into 3 to 4 chunks

3 celery stalks, cut into 3 to 4 chunks

2 large onions, quartered, or 1 large onion plus 4 to 5 leek greens

Large bunch of parsley stems

1 bay leaf

½ teaspoon dried thyme

1 teaspoon salt, or to taste

½ teaspoon whole black peppercorns

Place the shanks and remaining ingredients in the cooker. Add just enough water to cover by 1 inch.

Lock the lid in place and over high heat bring to high pressure. Adjust the heat to maintain high pressure and cook for 1 hour. Let the pressure drop naturally, about 30 minutes, or use a quick-release method. Remove the lid, tilting it away from you to allow steam to escape.

Allow the broth to cool slightly. Strain into a large storage container. Cover and refrigerate overnight. Remove the congealed fat from the top before using or freezing.

Chicken or Turkey Broth

You'll get a creditable chicken broth with a young (2½- to 3-pound) broiler, but half of a 5- or 6-pound stewing hen—if you can find one—will give you a better one; just freeze the second half until you're ready to prepare another batch of broth. The hen yields a richer broth and provides tasty meat for sandwiches or chicken salad. The après-broth meat of young fowl lacks flavor and is best used for making croquettes.

This broth can be refrigerated for 5 days and frozen for up to 4 months.

MAKES APPROXIMATELY 1½ QUARTS

(30 MINUTES UNDER HIGH PRESSURE)

2½ to 3 pounds stewing chicken, cut into 6 pieces, or 1 turkey
  carcass with some meat intact, cut into 6 to 8 pieces
2 celery stalks, cut into 3 to 4 chunks
2 large carrots, cut into 3 to 4 chunks
1 to 2 parsnips, cut into 3 to 4 chunks (optional)
1 large onion, coarsely chopped
A few leek greens (optional)
4 to 5 dried mushrooms (optional)
½ teaspoon whole black peppercorns
1 teaspoon salt, or to taste
Large bunch of parsley stems
1 bay leaf

Place all of the ingredients in the cooker. Add just enough water to cover by 1 inch.

Lock the lid in place and over high heat bring to high pressure. Adjust the heat to maintain high pressure and cook for 30 minutes. Let the pressure drop naturally, about 25 minutes, or use a quick-release method. Remove the lid, tilting it away from you to allow steam to escape.

Allow the broth to cool slightly. Strain into a large storage container. Cover and refrigerate overnight. Remove the congealed fat from the top before using or freezing.

Veal Broth

Veal broth is a superb alternative to chicken broth in soups and stews. Browning the onion builds in a bit more flavor, but you'll produce a fine broth even if you decide to skip that step.

This broth can be refrigerated for 5 days and frozen for up to 4 months.

MAKES APPROXIMATELY 1½ QUARTS

(45 MINUTES UNDER HIGH PRESSURE)

1 tablespoon oil
1 large onion, coarsely chopped
2 pounds veal bones
2 celery stalks, coarsely chopped
2 large carrots, coarsely chopped
1 medium white turnip, peeled and quartered (optional)
1/2 teaspoon whole black peppercorns
1 bay leaf
5 sprigs parsley
1/2 teaspoon dried thyme (optional)
1 teaspoon salt, or to taste

Heat the oil in the cooker and sauté the onion over medium heat until lightly browned, stirring frequently, 4 to 5 minutes. Add the remaining ingredients, with just enough water to cover by 1 inch. Scrape up any browned bits of onion sticking to the bottom of the pot.

Lock the lid in place and over high heat bring to high pressure. Adjust the heat to maintain high pressure and cook for 45 minutes. Let the pressure drop naturally, about 20 minutes, or use a quick-release method. Remove the lid, tilting it away from you to allow steam to escape.

Allow the broth to cool slightly. Strain into a large storage container. Cover and refrigerate overnight. Remove the congealed fat from the top before using or freezing.

Fish Broth

Try to use a variety of nonoily, white-fleshed fish heads and bones for broth. Remove all gills and wash away any blood (which imparts a bitter taste to the broth).

Since it is becoming increasingly difficult to get fish heads separately, ask for the head and bones when you buy fillets. Freeze them until you're ready to make this lovely broth.

This broth can be refrigerated for 3 days and frozen for up to 4 months.

MAKES APPROXIMATELY 1½ QUARTS

(15 MINUTES UNDER HIGH PRESSURE)

3 pounds fish heads and bones, thoroughly rinsed to remove all
  blood

1 large onion, coarsely chopped, or 1 large leek, thoroughly rinsed
  and thinly sliced

2 carrots, coarsely chopped

2 celery stalks, coarsely chopped

1 bay leaf

6 sprigs parsley

1/2 teaspoon dried thyme (optional)

6 whole black peppercorns

1 teaspoon salt, or to taste

Place all of the ingredients in the cooker plus enough water to cover by 1 inch.

Lock the lid in place and over high heat bring to high pressure. Adjust the heat to maintain high pressure and cook for 15 minutes. Let the pressure drop naturally, about 12 minutes, or use a quick-release method. Remove the lid, tilting it away from you to allow steam to escape.

Allow the broth to cool slightly. Strain into a large storage container. Cover and refrigerate or freeze until needed.

Vegetable Broth

The pressure cooker got me into the habit of preparing vegetable broth on a regular basis since the task requires no preplanning or fuss. For a more freeform approach, try the No-Fuss Vegetable Broth recipe (page 33). This broth is best when used within 2 to 3 days. It loses a good deal of flavor once it's been frozen.

MAKES APPROXIMATELY 1½ QUARTS

(10 MINUTES UNDER HIGH PRESSURE)

1 tablespoon oil

2 medium onions, coarsely chopped

1 to 2 garlic cloves, minced (optional)

3 large carrots, cut into 3 to 4 chunks

4 celery stalks, cut into 3 to 4 chunks

1 to 2 parsnips, cut into 3 to 4 chunks

2 bay leaves

1/2 teaspoon dried thyme or dried oregano

6 sprigs fresh parsley, cilantro, or basil

8 cups coarsely chopped miscellaneous vegetables (see Potential Candidates for the Vegetable Broth Pot, page 33)

1/2 teaspoon salt, or to taste

Heat the oil in the cooker and sauté the onions and garlic (if using) over medium heat, stirring frequently, until golden brown, 5 to 6 minutes. Toss in the carrots and celery and sauté an additional minute. Add the parsnips, bay leaves, thyme, parsley, chopped vegetables, salt, and just enough water to cover. Stir carefully to scrape up any browned bits of onion sticking to the bottom of the pot.

Lock the lid in place and over high heat bring to high pressure. Adjust the heat to maintain high pressure and cook for 10 minutes. Let the pressure drop naturally, 7 to 10 minutes, or use a quick-release method. Remove the lid, tilting it away from you to allow steam to escape.

Allow the broth to cool slightly. Strain into a large storage container. Cover and refrigerate until needed.

No-Fuss Vegetable Broth

The pressure cooker is the only pot I know that makes it possible for you to make a broth in the amount of time it takes to tidy up the kitchen after a bout of cooking.

While developing the recipes for this book, every day or two I would simply take my bagful of vegetable peelings and odd bits, rinse them off, pile them into the pressure cooker, and cover them with water. I would lock the lid in place, bring up to high pressure, and cook for about 5 minutes. I usually let the pressure drop naturally and strained the broth whenever I got around to it, but you can also use the quick-release method if you're in a hurry. Either way, you'll end up with a light broth that makes a pleasing soup base for the recipes that follow.

Be sure to scrub all vegetables well if you plan to use the peelings for broth. Avoid beets, onion and turnip peels, and cabbage, which either discolor the broth or simply give it too strong an aroma or flavor.

(5 MINUTES UNDER HIGH PRESSURE)

POTENTIAL CANDIDATES FOR THE VEGETABLE BROTH POT

Potato peelings

Broccoli stalks

Zucchini

Celery, parsnip, and carrot chunks, peelings, and trimmings

Wilted celery and carrots

Onions

Leek greens

Scallions

Parsley, dill, cilantro, and basil sprigs, leaves, or stems

Wilted lettuce and watercress

Turnips (always peel them)

Bay leaf or a few pinches of dried herbs (if you're feeling magnanimous)

☕ SOUPS ☕

In the soup recipes that follow, the liquid ingredient is usually some type of broth—chicken, beef, or vegetable—and the choice is yours. When I don't have any homemade broth on hand, I use a salt-free or lightly salted instant vegetable bouillon cube such as Morga (available in health-food stores) or a good-quality aseptic-packed chicken broth, such as Pacific brand. For backup, I keep beef and chicken Better Than Bouillon paste in the refrigerator. Since the latter brand is very salty, I use only ½ teaspoon paste per cup of water rather than the recommended 1 teaspoon.

Of course, there's nothing quite like the taste of a soup based on homemade broth, but the pressure cooker is so efficient at extracting every last ounce of taste from ingredients that soups emerge full-flavored and luscious even if you're using water or a light instant vegetable broth.

Borscht

There's no need to peel the beets for this hearty winter vegetable soup. A few parsnips bring out the sweetness of the beets. Serve with a dollop of sour cream, which adds a nice flavor contrast and dramatizes the brilliant crimson color.

SERVES 8

(10 MINUTES UNDER HIGH PRESSURE)

2 tablespoons unsalted butter

1 large onion, coarsely chopped

1 1/2 quarts (6 cups) beef or vegetable broth or bouillon

One 28-ounce can tomatoes, coarsely chopped, including juice

1 pound beets, scrubbed, trimmed, halved, and cut into 1/2-inch slices

1 pound cabbage, cored and shredded

3 large carrots, scrubbed or peeled and cut into 3 to 4 chunks

3 slender parsnips, peeled and cut into 3 to 4 chunks

3 bay leaves

1 tablespoon caraway seeds

1/2 teaspoon ground allspice

2 to 3 tablespoons red wine vinegar

Salt

Garnish: sour cream

Heat the butter in the cooker and sauté the onions until soft, stirring frequently, about 3 minutes. Add the remaining ingredients except the vinegar, salt, and sour cream.

Lock the lid in place and over high heat bring to high pressure. Adjust the heat to maintain high pressure and cook for 10 minutes. Let the pressure drop naturally or quick-release by placing the pot under cold running water. (Other quick-release methods are likely to cause sputtering.)

Remove the lid, tilting it away from you to allow steam to escape. Remove the bay leaves. Stir in vinegar and salt to taste. Garnish each portion with a dollop of sour cream.

New England Fish Chowder

This simple, thick, and very tasty chowder is done in a flash. Make it as rich as you like by stirring in either milk, half-and-half, or heavy cream at the end.

SERVES 4

(4 MINUTES UNDER HIGH PRESSURE, THEN 2–3 MINUTES SIMMERING)

2 tablespoons unsalted butter or oil

1 large onion, finely chopped

3 celery stalks, finely chopped

1 large carrot, finely chopped

1 pound potatoes, peeled and cut into 1/2-inch dice

1 pound thick firm-fleshed white fish fillets, such as cod, cut into
   1 1/2-inch chunks

2 cups fish broth or clam juice

1 cup water

1 bay leaf

1/2 teaspoon dried thyme

1 to 1 1/2 cups milk, half-and-half, or heavy cream

1 cup fresh or frozen corn kernels

1/4 cup finely chopped fresh parsley

Salt and freshly ground white or black pepper

Garnish: additional unsalted butter, cut into pats (optional)

Heat the butter in the cooker. Sauté the onions until soft, 2 to 3 minutes. Toss in the celery, carrot, and potatoes, and sauté an additional minute. Add the fish chunks, broth (watch for sputtering oil), water, bay leaf, and thyme.

Lock the lid in place and over high heat bring to high pressure. Adjust the heat to maintain high pressure and cook for 4 minutes. Reduce the pressure with a quick-release method. Remove the lid, tilting it away from you to allow steam to escape.

Stir in the milk, corn, parsley, and salt and pepper to taste. Simmer until the corn is cooked. Top individual servings with additional butter, if desired.

Scotch Broth

I like to thicken a classic Scottish lamb-and-barley soup with split peas, which virtually dissolve by the time the soup is cooked. Some versions of the soup add chunks of rutabaga and chopped cabbage, but this recipe is extremely flavorful without them. After only 20 minutes of cooking, lamb neck—an inexpensive underutilized cut, practically falls off the bone. No wonder the Scotch consider it soul food.

Try to prepare this soup a day in advance so that you can refrigerate it and remove the fat that congeals on the surface before serving.

SERVES 8

(20 MINUTES UNDER HIGH PRESSURE)

2¹/₂ pounds lamb neck, cut into 2-inch pieces and trimmed of excess fat

2 quarts (8 cups) water

¹/₂ teaspoon salt, or to taste

¹/₂ cup pearl barley, picked over and rinsed

¹/₂ cup split peas, picked over and rinsed

2 medium leeks, white part only, thoroughly rinsed and thinly sliced (about 1¹/₂ cups)

1 large onion, coarsely chopped

2 large carrots, scrubbed or peeled and cut into 3 to 4 chunks

2 celery stalks, finely chopped

2 bay leaves

4 to 5 sprigs parsley

Rinse the lamb and set it in the bottom of the cooker. Add the water and slowly bring to a boil. Skim off any solid white scum that forms on the surface. Add the salt and skim again. Add the remaining ingredients.

Lock the lid in place and over high heat bring to high pressure. Adjust the heat to maintain high pressure and cook for 20 minutes. Let the pressure drop naturally or use a quick-release method. Remove the lid, tilting it away from you to allow steam to escape.

Remove the bay leaves and parsley and add more salt, if desired.

Turkey-Vegetable Hot Pot

Before attempting to prepare this chunky soup, be sure two turkey drumsticks will fit into your cooker. Most cookers will hold them after a little imaginative juggling; there's no harm if the end of the bone touches the lid of the cooker, as long as it doesn't block the vent. Alternatively, you can use a drumstick and thigh.

SERVES 4

(12 MINUTES UNDER HIGH PRESSURE, THEN 3–5 MINUTES SIMMERING)

1 tablespoon olive oil

1 garlic clove, finely minced

1 cup chicken broth

One 35-ounce can tomatoes, coarsely chopped, including juice

1 1/2 pounds (about 8) small potatoes (preferably red or russet), scrubbed

2 large carrots, peeled and cut into 4 to 5 chunks

10 ounces (about 8) small white onions, peeled

3 celery stalks, finely chopped

1/3 cup (1/2 ounce) loosely packed dried mushrooms

1 teaspoon dried oregano

1/2 teaspoon dried rosemary leaves

2 bay leaves

1/2 teaspoon salt, or to taste

2 young turkey drumsticks (1 to 1 1/4 pounds each), or 1 drumstick and thigh (about 2 pounds total), skinned

10 ounces fresh or frozen (defrosted) green beans

1 1/2 cups fresh or frozen (defrosted) corn kernels

1/2 cup finely minced fresh parsley or cilantro

Salt and freshly ground black pepper

Heat the oil in the cooker and sauté the garlic for 10 seconds. Add the broth, tomatoes, potatoes, carrots, onions, celery, mushrooms, oregano, rosemary, bay leaves, and salt. Stand the two drumsticks, meaty side down, in the soup.

Lock the lid in place and over high heat bring to high pressure. Adjust the heat to maintain high pressure and cook for 12 minutes. Let the pressure drop naturally or use a quick-release method. Remove the lid, tilting it away from you to allow steam to escape.

Remove the drumsticks and set them on a cutting board. Stir the green beans, corn, and parsley into the cooker, and cook uncovered over medium heat until the vegetables are tender, 3 to 5 minutes.

Meanwhile, slice the turkey meat from the bones. Cut the meat into 1-inch chunks and return it to the pot. Discard the drumstick bones (or reserve them for broth). Remove the bay leaves, and add salt and pepper to taste.

Minestrone

This superb recipe combines the long-simmered flavors brought out by pressure cooking with the crunch of green beans, zucchini, and shredded cabbage added during a final simmer. The soup thickens considerably on standing; I often serve it as a stew or sauce over noodles or rice—or you can thin it with a bit of water or vegetable broth. In either case, stir well before serving, as the orzo tends to sink to the bottom. SERVES 8–10

(25 MINUTES UNDER HIGH PRESSURE, THEN 8–10 MINUTES SIMMERING)

2 tablespoons olive oil

2 garlic cloves, finely minced

1 large onion, coarsely chopped

3 large carrots, cut into 1/2-inch slices

1 medium leek, thoroughly rinsed and thinly sliced

3 celery stalks, cut into 1-inch slices

1 teaspoon dried thyme or dried oregano

3/4 cup dried navy (pea) beans, picked over and rinsed

3 cups water

3 cups vegetable broth or bouillon, plus more if needed

One 14-ounce can Italian plum tomatoes, including juice

6 ounces green beans, trimmed and cut into thirds (about 2 cups loosely packed)

1/2 cup orzo, tubettini, or other small Italian pasta

2 large zucchini, cut into 1/2-inch slices

3 cups loosely packed, cored, shredded cabbage

1 teaspoon salt, or to taste

Freshly ground black pepper

1/2 cup tightly packed minced fresh basil or Italian (flat-leaf) parsley, divided

Garnish: 1 to 1 1/2 cups grated Parmesan or romano

Heat the olive oil in the cooker and sauté the garlic and onion until the onion becomes limp, about 3 minutes. Add the carrots, leek, celery, thyme, navy beans, water, and broth.

Lock the lid in place and over high heat bring to high pressure. Adjust the heat to maintain high pressure and cook for 25 minutes. Let the pressure drop naturally or use a quick-release method. Remove the lid, tilting it away from you to allow steam to escape. If the beans aren't close to tender, return to high pressure and cook for another 5 minutes.

Add the tomatoes, green beans, and orzo, and cook uncovered over medium heat for 5 minutes, stirring frequently so that the orzo doesn't drop to the bottom of the pot and burn. If the soup becomes too thick, add 1 to 2 cups more broth.

Add the zucchini, cabbage, and salt and pepper to taste. Cook until the zucchini and green beans are crisp-tender, 3 to 5 additional minutes. Stir in the basil. Serve in individual bowls, garnished with Parmesan or romano.

NOTE: For a friend of mine, a superb minestrone always contains one secret ingredient: a tablespoon of sugar to enhance all of the flavors. She may be right.

Mushroom-Barley Soup

I always used to schedule my trips to New York City's Lower East Side on days that the much beloved Ratner's Dairy Restaurant served its famous mushroom-barley soup. Accompanied by a shameful number of onion rolls slathered with sweet butter, it made the world's best winter lunch. Now that Ratner's is gone, it's especially nostalgic for me to enjoy this delicious adaptation of their recipe.

If your vegetable broth is heavily salted, soak the dried baby lima beans overnight to ensure proper cooking. Don't use large limas in this recipe, as they have different cooking requirements. SERVES 8–10

(22–25 MINUTES UNDER HIGH PRESSURE)

2 tablespoons unsalted butter or oil

1 to 2 large garlic cloves, minced

2 cups coarsely chopped onions

1 small leek, thoroughly rinsed and thinly sliced (optional)

2 quarts (8 cups) vegetable broth, preferably unsalted

1 cup loosely packed dried mushrooms (1 1/2 ounces; see Note)

3 celery stalks, thinly sliced

3 large carrots, coarsely chopped

2 to 3 medium parsnips, coarsely chopped

1 green bell pepper, seeded and coarsely chopped

1/2 cup dried baby lima beans, picked over and rinsed

1/2 cup pearl barley, picked over and rinsed

1/2 pound fresh mushrooms, quartered

2 bay leaves

1/2 cup finely minced fresh dill

1/2 teaspoon salt, or to taste

Heat the butter in the cooker. Sauté the garlic, onions, and optional leek, stirring frequently, until the onions are golden brown, 4 to 5 minutes. Stir in the remaining ingredients except the dill and salt. Make certain that no bits of onion or garlic are sticking to the bottom of the cooker.

Lock the lid in place and over high heat bring to high pressure. Ad-

just the heat to maintain high pressure, and cook for 22 minutes. Let the pressure drop naturally or use a quick-release method. Remove the lid, tilting it away from you to allow steam to escape. Discard the bay leaves and stir in the dill. Add salt and serve.

NOTE: It's nice to use 4 to 5 dried porcini mushrooms along with the dried mushrooms readily available in supermarkets. Although expensive, they add an intense earthy flavor to the soup.

Pureed Zucchini Soup
This simple and delicious recipe was created by my friend and neighbor Judy Bloom, whose ongoing enthusiasm for pressure cookery has inspired many of my own inventions.

SERVES 4–6

(5 MINUTES UNDER HIGH PRESSURE)

2 tablespoons olive oil

1 large onion, coarsely chopped

2 large garlic cloves, crushed

2 small potatoes (1/2 pound), scrubbed, halved, and cut into 1-inch chunks

2 large carrots, cut into 1/2-inch slices

4 large zucchini (2 pounds), cut into 1-inch chunks

4 cups vegetable broth or bouillon

1/2 teaspoon crushed red pepper flakes

1/3 cup chopped fresh basil or parsley

Salt and freshly ground black pepper

Heat the oil in the cooker. Sauté the onions and garlic for 1 minute. Add the potatoes and sauté for another 1 to 2 minutes. Add the carrots, zucchini, broth, and crushed red pepper flakes.

Lock the lid in place and over high heat bring to high pressure. Adjust the heat to maintain high pressure and cook for 5 minutes. Let the pressure drop naturally or use a quick-release method. Remove the lid, tilting it away from you to allow steam to escape.

Stir in the basil, reserving a few tablespoons for garnish. Use an immersion blender to puree the soup. Adjust the seasonings and serve each portion with a sprinkling of basil.

Lima Bean–Vegetable Soup

Here is a quick and simple soup for lovers of limas, which cook amazingly quickly under pressure. Be sure to use large limas, as they cook more quickly than baby limas and have a starchy, silken texture.

SERVES 6

(16–18 MINUTES UNDER HIGH PRESSURE)

2 tablespoons olive oil

2 cups coarsely chopped onion

4 celery stalks, thinly sliced

5 large carrots, cut into 5 to 6 chunks

4 large parsnips, cut into 3 to 4 chunks

2 cups dried large lima beans, picked over and rinsed

4 cups vegetable or chicken broth or bouillon

4 cups water

$1/3$ cup loosely packed dried mushrooms ($1/2$ ounce)

1 teaspoon dried oregano or dried thyme

$1/2$ cup finely minced fresh parsley

Salt and freshly ground black pepper

Heat the oil in the cooker. Add the onion and celery, and sauté for 2 minutes, stirring frequently. Add the carrots, parsnips, lima beans, broth, water, mushrooms, and oregano.

Lock the lid in place and over high heat bring to high pressure. Adjust the heat to maintain high pressure and cook for 16 minutes. Let the pressure drop naturally or use a quick-release method. Remove the lid, tilting it away from you to allow steam to escape.

Stir in the parsley and season with salt and pepper to taste.

Potato Soup with Onions and Cheddar

Pressure cooking makes the act of peeling potatoes obsolete since the skins become very tender and infuse the broth with earthy flavor.

SERVES 6

(5 MINUTES UNDER HIGH PRESSURE, THEN 2–3 MINUTES SIMMERING)

2 tablespoons unsalted butter or oil

1 garlic clove, finely minced

4 celery stalks, thinly sliced

3 scallions, thinly sliced

10 ounces pearl onions, peeled

2 pounds potatoes (preferably Maine or russet), scrubbed, halved, and cut into 1/4-inch slices

6 cups beef, chicken, or vegetable broth or bouillon

1/2 cup finely minced fresh parsley

1/2 cup milk (optional)

1 cup grated sharp Cheddar

Salt and freshly ground white pepper

Heat the butter in the cooker. Sauté the garlic, celery, and scallions for a minute or two. Stir in the onions and potatoes, tossing to coat with the butter. Add the broth.

Lock the lid in place and over high heat bring to high pressure. Adjust the heat to maintain high pressure and cook for 5 minutes. Let the pressure drop naturally or use a quick-release method. Remove the lid, tilting it away from you to allow steam to escape.

Add the parsley and milk (if using). Over low heat, gradually stir in the grated cheese, simmering until the cheese is melted and the soup is hot. Add salt and pepper to taste before serving.

Sweet Potato Soup
In the "pc," sweet potatoes melt down in a flash to give this colorful soup wholesome body and a luscious texture.

SERVES 6–8

(4 MINUTES UNDER HIGH PRESSURE)

2 tablespoons unsalted butter or oil

1 medium onion, finely chopped

3 celery stalks, thinly sliced

5 sweet potatoes (about 2 pounds), peeled and coarsely chopped

2 large McIntosh apples, peeled, cored, and coarsely chopped

5 cups chicken or vegetable broth or bouillon

1 to 1 1/2 teaspoons grated orange zest

1/2 teaspoon salt, or to taste

Heat the butter in the cooker. Sauté the onions until soft, about 3 minutes. Add the celery and sweet potatoes, and toss to coat with the butter. Stir in the apples and broth.

Lock the lid in place and over high heat bring to high pressure. Adjust the heat to maintain high pressure and cook for 4 minutes. Let the pressure drop naturally or use a quick-release method. Remove the lid, tilting it away from you to allow steam to escape.

Stir in the orange zest and salt. If the soup seems too thin, use an immersion blender to puree some of the sweet potatoes.

Beet Soup with Beet Greens and Sweet Potatoes

A soup that sports all the colors of a brilliant autumn day. Since sweet potatoes cook more quickly than beets, cut them into thicker slices, which are more likely to keep their shape. The beet greens add a very appealing spinachlike flavor.

The pressure cooker does a thorough job of tenderizing beet skins, so peeling the beets is more a matter of aesthetics than necessity.

SERVES 6

(7 MINUTES UNDER HIGH PRESSURE)

5 medium beets, with greens attached

3 medium sweet potatoes (about 1 1/2 pounds), peeled

2 tablespoons unsalted butter or oil

1 large onion, coarsely chopped

6 cups vegetable broth or bouillon

1 teaspoon grated orange zest

1 to 2 teaspoons finely minced fresh ginger

1/2 teaspoon salt, or to taste

Cut the beets from their greens and peel or scrub them. Halve the beets and cut each half into thin slices. Set aside.

Cut and discard the red stems from the beet greens. Rinse the beet greens in a sinkful of cold water, taking care to remove all of the sand. Discard any blemished or very large, tough leaves. Drain and chop the beet greens into strips about 2 inches wide. Use about 4 cups of tightly packed chopped greens for the soup, saving the remainder for broth or another use. (They're delicious when sautéed in olive oil with lots of garlic.)

Cut the peeled sweet potatoes in half lengthwise and cut each half into 1/2-inch slices.

Heat the butter in the cooker. Add the onions and cook until soft, about 3 minutes. Add the beet greens, sliced beets, sweet potatoes, and broth.

Lock the lid in place and over high heat bring to high pressure. Adjust the heat to maintain high pressure and cook for 7 minutes. Reduce the pressure with a quick-release method. Remove the lid, tilting it away from you to allow steam to escape.

Stir in the orange zest, ginger, and salt.

Curried Parsnip Soup

I've never understood why parsnips get so little attention; they're so sweet and mellow. Perhaps it's the relatively long cooking time that discourages people—a circumstance rendered obsolete by the pressure cooker. Since large, fat parsnips tend to be woody, look for the slenderest ones you can find.

Rolled oats add a creamy richness to the soup. For an informal meal, puree half of the soup, leaving some parsnip chunks intact for texture. For a more elegant version, puree the whole batch. In either case, set a dollop of cilantro-ginger yogurt on top of each portion.　　SERVES 4–6

(6 MINUTES UNDER HIGH PRESSURE)

1¹/₂ pounds parsnips, preferably slender ones

2 tablespoons unsalted butter or oil

2 to 3 teaspoons finely minced fresh ginger

1 tablespoon mild curry powder

4 celery stalks, cut into ¹/₂-inch slices

4 cups vegetable or chicken broth or bouillon

¹/₂ cup old-fashioned rolled oats

Salt

1 cup yogurt

¹/₄ cup chopped cilantro

1¹/₂ teaspoons grated fresh ginger

1 tablespoon freshly squeezed lime juice

Peel, trim and cut the parsnips into ¹/₂-inch slices. Cut large tops into 2 to 3 chunks. (You should have about 4 cups of chopped parsnips.)

Heat the butter in the cooker. Add the ginger and curry powder, stirring constantly for 5 seconds. Add the celery, parsnips, broth, oats, and salt to taste.

Lock the lid in place and over high heat bring to high pressure. Adjust the heat to maintain high pressure and cook for 6 minutes. Let the pressure drop naturally or use a quick-release method. Remove the lid, tilting it away from you to allow steam to escape.

While the soup is cooking, prepare the yogurt topping by combining the yogurt, cilantro, ginger, and lime juice.

Puree all or part of the soup with an immersion blender. Adjust the seasonings. Serve each portion with a dollop of the yogurt topping.

Lentil Soup with Prunes and Pears

An elegant and dressed-up version of an old favorite. The lentils become soft and puffy but retain their shape, as do the chunks of prunes and pears. These sweet fruits mask the typically peppery flavor of lentils in a most appealing way.

The thickness of the soup is somewhat unpredictable; use a bit of water or broth to thin it, if necessary.

For a very simple and more conventional lentil soup recipe, see page 209.   SERVES 6–8

(20 MINUTES UNDER HIGH PRESSURE)

1 tablespoon unsalted butter or oil
2 cups dried lentils, picked over and rinsed
1/2 cup pearl barley, picked over and rinsed
6 cups water
1 teaspoon ground coriander
1/4 teaspoon ground cloves
1 cup pitted prunes, halved
3 ripe pears, peeled, cored, and cut into large chunks
1 teaspoon salt, or to taste

Heat the butter in the cooker and stir in the lentils and barley. Add the remaining ingredients except the salt.

Lock the lid in place and over high heat bring to high pressure. Adjust the heat to maintain high pressure and cook for 20 minutes. Let the pressure drop naturally or use a quick-release method. Remove the lid, tilting it away from you to allow steam to escape. Add salt and serve.

Black Bean Soup

A smoked ham hock or pig's knuckle gives this soup an appealing smoky flavor, but you can omit it for a vegetarian version.

SERVES 8

(35–40 MINUTES UNDER HIGH PRESSURE)

2 tablespoons olive oil
1 tablespoon whole cumin seeds (yes, 1 tablespoon!)
2 large garlic cloves, minced
2 large onions, coarsely chopped
4 celery stalks, cut into chunks
1 large green bell pepper, seeded and diced
6 cups water
1 smoked ham hock or pig's knuckle (optional)
3 large carrots, peeled and cut into chunks
2 bay leaves
1 teaspoon dried thyme
1 1/2 cups dried black beans, picked over and rinsed
1 cup tightly packed, minced fresh cilantro
1 to 2 teaspoons salt

Heat the oil in the cooker. Add the cumin, stirring constantly for 5 seconds. Add the garlic and onions, and sauté until the onions are soft, about 3 minutes. Add the remaining ingredients except the fresh cilantro and salt.

Lock the lid in place and over high heat bring to high pressure. Adjust the heat to maintain high pressure and cook for 35 minutes. Let the pressure drop naturally or use a quick-release method. Remove the lid, tilting it away from you to allow steam to escape.

Remove the bay leaves and ham hock (if using). Stir in the cilantro and salt to taste. The soup thickens on standing, but if you wish to serve it immediately and it is too thin, puree about a cupful of the cooked beans and stir them back in.

Nutty Carrot Soup

This soup has an autumn-orange color and a nutty richness, thanks to the addition of a little peanut butter at the end.

SERVES 6–8

(5 MINUTES UNDER HIGH PRESSURE)

2 tablespoons unsalted butter or oil

3 celery stalks, cut into 1/4-inch slices

1 pound carrots, scrubbed, trimmed, and cut into 1/4-inch slices

2 medium apples, such as McIntosh, peeled, cored, and chopped

1 large potato (about 1/2 pound), scrubbed, halved lengthwise, and cut into 1/4-inch slices

5 cups water

1/4 cup peanut, cashew, or almond butter

1 teaspoon salt, or to taste

Freshly ground black pepper and grated nutmeg

Heat the butter in the cooker. Add the celery, carrots, apples, and potato, and sauté for 1 minute. Stir in the water.

Lock the lid in place and over high heat bring to high pressure. Adjust the heat to maintain high pressure and cook for 5 minutes. Reduce the pressure with a quick-release method. Remove the lid, tilting it away from you to allow steam to escape.

Puree the soup with an immersion blender or in batches in a standard blender or food processor. Blend in the nut butter. Reheat if necessary. Season to taste with salt, pepper, and nutmeg before serving.

Cabbage Soup with Caraway
The combination of apple cider, tomatoes, and vinegar gives this soup an intriguing sweet-and-sour taste. Serve it with a salad and some hearty, whole-grain bread for a simple and satisfying supper. SERVES 8–10

(5 MINUTES UNDER HIGH PRESSURE)

2 tablespoons unsalted butter or oil

1 cup coarsely chopped onions

1 tablespoon caraway seeds

2 bay leaves

2 cups apple cider

2 cups vegetable broth or bouillon

2 cups cold water

2 tablespoons apple cider vinegar

2/3 cup uncooked white rice

1 medium head cabbage (about 2 pounds), quartered, cored, and
   shredded

2 tablespoons tomato paste

One 28-ounce can tomatoes, coarsely chopped,
   including juice

1 teaspoon salt, or to taste

Freshly ground black pepper to taste

Heat the butter in the cooker. Sauté the onions and caraway seeds until the onions are soft, about 3 minutes. Add the remaining ingredients in the order listed. *Do not stir.*

Lock the lid in place and over high heat bring to high pressure. Adjust the heat to maintain high pressure and cook for 5 minutes. Reduce the pressure with a quick-release method. Remove the lid, tilting it away from you to allow steam to escape.

Stir well and discard the bay leaves. Adjust the seasonings and serve.

Creamy Leek and Potato Soup

For a more elegant version of this rustic country soup, puree the entire mixture—but don't overprocess or the potatoes will become gummy.

SERVES 6

(5 MINUTES UNDER HIGH PRESSURE)

3 tablespoons unsalted butter

6 medium leeks, white and light green parts, thoroughly rinsed, and thinly sliced (about 4 cups)

3 celery stalks, thinly sliced

3 large potatoes (about 1 1/2 pounds), peeled and cut into small chunks

5 cups vegetable or chicken broth or bouillon

1/4 cup finely minced fresh dill (optional)

Salt and freshly ground black pepper

Heat the butter in the cooker. Sauté the leeks and celery for 2 minutes, stirring occasionally. Add the potatoes and broth.

Lock the lid in place and over high heat bring to high pressure. Adjust the heat to maintain high pressure and cook for 5 minutes. Let the pressure drop naturally or use a quick-release method. Remove the lid, tilting it away from you to allow steam to escape.

Puree half of the soup in a blender or food processor. Pour the puree back into the pot. Stir in the dill (if desired) and add salt and pepper to taste. Reheat thoroughly and serve.

Split-Pea Soup with Sweet Potatoes and Mint

Most pressure cooker manufacturers consider split peas a "forbidden food," as they have a tendency to foam while cooking and can clog the vent. By coating the peas with oil or butter and by putting a carefully calculated amount of liquid in the cooker (never filling it above the halfway point), I have experienced no problems whatsoever.

This soup is very thick and can be served as is or thinned with a few additional cups of vegetable broth. The sweet potatoes and apples lend a fresh and sweet flavor. Two teaspoons of dried mint give the soup a "hint of mint"; three strongly flavor it.   SERVES 6–8

(10 MINUTES UNDER HIGH PRESSURE, THEN 10 MINUTES FOR NATURAL PRESSURE RELEASE)

2 tablespoons unsalted butter or oil

1 large onion, coarsely chopped

3 celery stalks, sliced

2 cups dried split peas, picked over and rinsed

4 cups water

4 cups vegetable or chicken broth or bouillon

2 medium sweet potatoes (12 ounces), peeled and cut into chunks

2 large, sweet apples, such as McIntosh, peeled, cored, and cut into eighths

1 bay leaf

2 to 3 teaspoons dried mint

1 teaspoon salt, or to taste

Heat the butter in the cooker. Sauté the onion, stirring frequently, until golden brown, 4 to 5 minutes. Add the celery and split peas, stirring to coat with the fat.

Add the water plus 2 cups of the broth, making sure to scrape up any bits of onion that are stuck to the bottom of the pot. Add the sweet potatoes, apples, bay leaf, and mint.

Lock the lid in place and over high heat bring to high pressure.

Adjust the heat to maintain high pressure and cook for 10 minutes. Let the pressure drop naturally, about 10 minutes. Remove the lid, tilting it away from you to allow steam to escape.

Stir well to blend the ingredients. Remove the bay leaf and add salt before serving.

Celery Soup with Aniseeds
This recipe puts celery in the limelight. The inventive and irresistible idea of adding aniseeds to celery soup comes from Felipe Rojas-Lombardi's Soup, Beautiful Soup. *This recipe is as simple to prepare as it is delicious.* SERVES 6

(3 MINUTES UNDER HIGH PRESSURE)

2 tablespoons unsalted butter or oil
1 tablespoon aniseeds
2 medium leeks, white part only, thoroughly rinsed, and thinly
   sliced (about 1 1/2 cups)
1 head celery (1 1/2 pounds), including leaves, cut into 1/2-inch slices
5 cups chicken or vegetable broth or bouillon
2/3 cup uncooked orzo
Salt

Heat the butter in the cooker. Sauté the aniseeds for 10 seconds, stirring constantly. Add the leeks and sauté for 2 minutes, stirring frequently. Stir in the celery, broth, and orzo.

Lock the lid in place and over high heat bring to high pressure. Adjust the heat to maintain high pressure and cook for 3 minutes. Reduce the pressure with a quick-release method. Remove the lid, tilting it away from you to allow steam to escape.

If the orzo or celery is not quite done, cook over medium heat, uncovered, for another minute or two. With a slotted spoon, remove about a third of the celery and orzo. Puree in a food processor or blender, then stir back into the soup. Reheat if necessary. Add salt to taste and serve immediately.

Broccoli-Corn Chowder

Here's a good way to enjoy those leftover stalks of broccoli after you've put the florets to some other use.

SERVES 6

(4 MINUTES UNDER HIGH PRESSURE)

2 tablespoons unsalted butter or oil

2 medium leeks, white part only, thoroughly rinsed and thinly sliced (about 1 1/2 cups)

1 medium onion, coarsely chopped

2 large potatoes (1 pound), peeled and cut into 1-inch chunks

Stalks from 2 heads broccoli (about 3/4 pound), peeled and coarsely chopped

5 cups vegetable broth

1/2 teaspoon salt, or to taste

1 cup fresh or frozen corn kernels

1/4 cup finely chopped fresh parsley

1/2 cup milk or half-and-half

Melt the butter in the cooker. Sauté the leeks and onion, stirring frequently, until the onion is lightly browned, about 4 minutes. Stir in the potatoes, broccoli, broth, and salt.

Lock the lid in place and over high heat bring to high pressure. Adjust the heat to maintain high pressure and cook for 4 minutes. Reduce the pressure with a quick-release method. Remove the lid, tilting it away from you to allow steam to escape.

Stir in the corn, parsley, and milk. Simmer until the corn is tender, 1 to 2 minutes. Adjust the seasonings before serving.

Quick Black-Eyed Pea Soup

Black-eyed peas don't get enough attention; their earthy flavor and mellow texture are absolutely superb. Since they cook very quickly, you can have this tasty soup on the table about 15 minutes after the idea comes to mind.

SERVES 6

(10 MINUTES UNDER HIGH PRESSURE, THEN 3–4 MINUTES SIMMERING)

2 tablespoons olive oil

1 large onion, coarsely chopped

1 large garlic clove, finely minced

2 cups dried black-eyed peas, picked over and rinsed

6 cups chicken, beef, or vegetable broth or bouillon

1 smoked ham hock (optional)

3 large carrots, trimmed (leave whole)

10 ounces frozen (defrosted) sliced okra

Tabasco or cayenne pepper to taste (optional)

Salt

Heat the oil in the cooker; sauté the onion and garlic until the onion is lightly browned, about 4 minutes. Add the peas, broth, ham hock (if using), and carrots. Lock the lid in place and over high heat bring to high pressure. Adjust the heat to maintain high pressure and cook for 10 minutes. Let the pressure drop naturally or use a quick-release method. Remove the lid, tilting it away from you to allow steam to escape.

Add the okra and remove the ham hock. Cut off the meat and stir it into the soup along with the Tabasco (if using) and salt to taste. Slash the carrots into chunks with a knife. Simmer until the okra is cooked, 3 to 4 minutes. Adjust the seasonings and serve.

Meat *and* Chicken

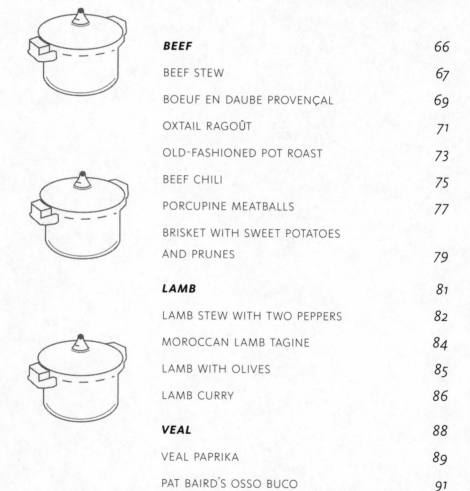

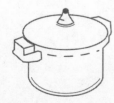

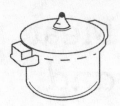

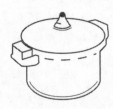

P ot roasts and stews are back in the limelight. These back-of-the-stove, long-simmering dishes are what traditional home cooking is all about. The pressure cooker catapults them to the front of the stove and onto your table in no time flat. Within moments, inexpensive cuts of meat emerge from the cooker as tender, moist morsels, full of character and intense flavor. Timeless classics such as coq au vin (9 minutes), chili (15 minutes), and lamb stew (15 minutes) can once again join your regular repertoire as quick-and-easy one-pot dinners rather than extravaganzas of preplanning and endless cooking.

Because the cooker extracts every last ounce of flavor from meat, an initial browning is unnecessary in many of the recipes that follow. In addition to saving time, skipping the browning stage eliminates the need to add extra fat. As a result, many of these recipes are more healthful but equally scrumptious versions of Grandma's best. See if you agree.

The range of recommended cooking times allows for the diversity in age and tenderness of ingredients as well as differences among cookers. Generally, meat will be properly cooked after the minimum time, but if more cooking is required, either return the cooker to high pressure for a few more minutes or cover and simmer with the lid unlocked.

Portion size? A particularly tricky issue in this chapter. I've given estimates for average-size servings, but please be forewarned: Pressure-cooked meats are so tender and full of flavor that most people can't resist taking second helpings.

The recipes in this chapter are delicious straight out of the pot, but like many dishes with multiple ingredients, the flavors deepen with overnight refrigeration. They can also be successfully frozen for up to 4 months.

⊜ BEEF ⊜

Generally, pressure-cooked beef chuck and round are transformed in a mere 16 to 20 minutes to moist and tender morsels; but as any aficionado knows, stewing meat occasionally can be tenaciously tough. If your stew is still chewy after 20 minutes, don't hesitate to give it another 5 to 10 minutes under pressure, adding a bit more broth to the pot if the mixture looks dry.

When cooking beef *it is essential* to let the pressure drop naturally to achieve fork-tender meat. Quick-releasing often results in tough, dry, and stringy meat. If you're in a hurry, quick-release any residual pressure only after you've let the pressure drop naturally for 10 minutes.

Beef Stew

This simple stew has no extra fat or fuss. Parsnips add a sweet accent; if they're unavailable, try peeled chunked turnips or winter squash instead.

The gravy is thickened in part by the coarsely chopped potatoes, which virtually disintegrate during cooking.

SERVES 4–6

(16–20 MINUTES UNDER HIGH PRESSURE, THEN 10 MINUTES FOR NATURAL PRESSURE RELEASE, THEN 4–5 MINUTES SIMMERING)

2 pounds (about 16) medium new potatoes, scrubbed
1 cup beef broth or bouillon
1 tablespoon Worcestershire sauce
2 bay leaves
1 1/2 teaspoons dried thyme
1 teaspoon dry mustard
1/8 teaspoon ground allspice
2 1/2 pounds beef stew meat, cut into 1 1/2-inch cubes, trimmed of excess fat
3/4 pound (about 9) small white onions, peeled (frozen are fine)
3 large carrots, trimmed, peeled, and cut into 3 to 4 chunks
3/4 pound parsnips, peeled, trimmed, and cut into thirds
3/4 pound mushrooms, quartered
One 14-ounce can tomatoes, coarsely chopped, including juice
1 cup frozen petit peas or green beans
1/4 cup finely chopped fresh parsley
1/2 teaspoon salt, or to taste
Freshly ground black pepper
1 tablespoon cornstarch (optional)

Coarsely chop 4 of the potatoes. Pour the broth into the cooker. Stir in the Worcestershire sauce, bay leaves, thyme, mustard, and allspice. Add the chopped and whole potatoes, beef, onions, carrots, parsnips, and mushrooms. Pour the tomatoes on top. *Do not stir.*

Lock the lid in place and over high heat bring to high pressure. Ad-

just the heat to maintain high pressure and cook for 16 minutes. Let the pressure drop naturally, about 10 minutes. *Do not use a quick-release method.* Remove the lid, tilting it away from you to allow steam to escape.

Test the beef for doneness. If it is not sufficiently tender, lock the lid back into place and return to high pressure for a few more minutes. Again, let the pressure drop naturally.

Remove the bay leaves. Stir in the peas and parsley. Add salt and pepper to taste. Simmer, stirring occasionally, until the vegetables are tender, about 1 minute for peas and 4 to 5 minutes for green beans. If the stew is too thin, dissolve the cornstarch in 1 tablespoon of water and add this mixture along with the peas. Simmer, stirring frequently, until the sauce thickens. Adjust the seasonings before serving.

Boeuf en Daube Provençal

A popular French version of beef stew, daube refers to the daubière, or covered casserole, in which it is traditionally simmered for 3 to 4 hours—a far cry from 16 minutes in the pressure cooker.

Marinating in wine overnight enhances the flavor of the meat, but is not essential; you can simply set all the ingredients in the cooker and be eating the stew within half an hour.

Serve with boiled potatoes, noodles, or rice. SERVES 4-6

(16–20 MINUTES UNDER HIGH PRESSURE, THEN 10 MINUTES FOR NATURAL PRESSURE RELEASE)

2 cups drinking-quality dry red wine

2 garlic cloves, chopped

1/2 teaspoon dried thyme

2 bay leaves

2 tablespoons tomato paste

3 to 5 anchovy fillets, packed in olive oil, drained, and mashed (optional)

2 1/2 pounds boneless chuck or round, cut into 1 1/2-inch cubes, trimmed of excess fat

2 tablespoons olive oil

1 large onion, sliced

1/3 cup pitted black olives, preferably oil-cured (optional)

1/2 teaspoon salt, or to taste

Freshly ground black pepper

4 large carrots, peeled (leave whole)

1/4 cup finely chopped fresh parsley

1 tablespoon cornstarch

Combine the wine, garlic, thyme, bay leaves, tomato paste, and mashed anchovies (if using) in a large nonaluminum bowl or storage container. Add the beef, cover, and refrigerate for a few hours or overnight.

Heat the oil in the cooker. Add the onion and cook over medium-high heat until lightly browned, about 4 minutes. Holding the beef cubes to one side, pour the wine marinade into the cooker and boil over high heat until it reduces somewhat, about 5 minutes.

Add the beef and stir in the olives (if using) plus salt (you are likely to need more if you haven't used the olives and anchovies) and pepper to taste. Set the carrots on top.

Lock the lid in place and over high heat bring to high pressure. Adjust the heat to maintain high pressure and cook for 16 minutes. Let the pressure drop naturally, about 10 minutes. *Do not use a quick-release method.* Remove the lid, tilting it away from you to allow steam to escape.

Test the beef for doneness. If it is not sufficiently tender, lock the lid back into place and return to high pressure for a few more minutes. Again, let the pressure drop naturally.

Slash the carrots into chunks. Stir in the parsley. To thicken the sauce, dissolve the cornstarch in 1 tablespoon of water and stir it in. Boil gently, stirring occasionally, until the mixture thickens, 1 to 2 minutes. Remove the bay leaves and adjust the seasonings before serving.

Oxtail Ragoût

I always associate oxtails with England, since this very traditional dish represents my first culinary taste of the British Isles. That oxtail stew was popular during the forties and fifties in America is evidenced by its inclusion in a rather brief selection of pressure cooker recipes published in the 1950 edition of The Joy of Cooking. *Back in the fifties, folks apparently knew what comfort food was all about.*

This stew is prepared in two parts. First the oxtails are cooked and the pressure is released. Then the vegetables are added for 5 more minutes of cooking under pressure. Unlike other cuts of beef, oxtails do not get tough when the quick release is used.

Serve the stew with mashed potatoes, rice, or barley to absorb the plentiful gravy. If your schedule permits, cook the oxtails a day or two before, cool and refrigerate, then remove the congealed fat from the top. Alternatively, pour the cooking liquid into a gravy separator and return the defatted broth to the cooker.

SERVES 4

(55–60 MINUTES UNDER HIGH PRESSURE (OXTAILS), THEN 5 MINUTES UNDER HIGH PRESSURE (VEGETABLES))

2 to 4 tablespoons oil

3 pounds oxtails, joints cut into 2-inch lengths and trimmed of excess fat

1 large onion, chopped

2 large garlic cloves, minced

2 celery stalks, finely chopped

One 12-ounce bottle Guinness stout

1 1/2 cups beef broth or bouillon, or water

1 tablespoon tomato paste

1/2 teaspoon dried thyme

1/2 teaspoon dry mustard

1 bay leaf

3/4 pound small white turnips, peeled and halved

2 large carrots, peeled and cut into 2-inch chunks

1 pound (about 12) small white onions, peeled (frozen is fine)

1 tablespoon cornstarch (optional)

1/2 teaspoon salt, or to taste (less if using salty broth or bouillon)

Heat 2 tablespoons of the oil in the cooker. Over high heat, brown the oxtails on all sides, in 2 to 3 batches, adding extra oil as needed. Transfer the browned oxtails to a platter and set aside.

Sauté the onions and garlic in the fat remaining in the pot, stirring frequently, until the onions are browned, 4 to 5 minutes. Return the browned oxtails to the cooker and stir in the remaining ingredients except the turnips, carrots, small onions, cornstarch, and salt. Make certain that there are no bits of onion sticking to the bottom of the cooker.

Lock the lid in place and over high heat bring to high pressure. Adjust the heat to maintain high pressure and cook for 55 minutes. Reduce the pressure naturally or use a quick-release method (which will not toughen the oxtails). Remove the lid, tilting it away from you to allow steam to escape.

At this point, the meat should be very tender, falling easily away from the bone when poked with a fork. If not, lock the lid back in place and return to high pressure for an additional 5 minutes. If time permits, refrigerate overnight and remove the congealed fat. Otherwise, use a gravy separator to defat the gravy.

About 20 minutes before you plan to serve, pour the broth surrounding the oxtails into the cooker. If it is very thick, add a little water. Stir in the turnips, carrots, and small onions. Lock the lid in place and over high heat bring to high pressure. Adjust the heat to maintain high pressure and cook for 5 minutes. Release the pressure with a quick-release method. Remove the lid, tilting it away from you to allow steam to escape.

Return the oxtails to the cooker. If you wish to thicken the stew, dissolve the cornstarch in 1 tablespoon of water. Stir in and simmer, stirring frequently, until the stew reaches the desired consistency. Add salt to taste before serving.

Old-fashioned Pot Roast

One of the most dramatic feats that the pressure cooker can perform is this roast: a fork-tender, melt-in-the-mouth piece of meat in an hour, with succulent vegetables to boot. Instead of browning the meat—a messy, steamy job in the "pc"—I like to roll it in a little soy sauce to give it good color and enhance flavor. The cooked roast, either whole or sliced, freezes well.

SERVES 4–6

(45–50 MINUTES UNDER HIGH PRESSURE, THEN 10–15 MINUTES FOR NATURAL PRESSURE RELEASE (POT ROAST), THEN 5 MINUTES UNDER HIGH PRESSURE (VEGETABLES))

1 to 2 tablespoons soy sauce

3 to 3 1/2 pounds beef chuck or round, trimmed of excess fat

2 to 4 garlic cloves, peeled

Freshly ground black pepper to taste

2 tablespoons canola or safflower oil

1/2 cup chopped celery

1 cup chopped carrot

1 cup chopped onion

2 cups beef broth or bouillon

2 bay leaves

1 teaspoon dried thyme

1 pound (about 12) small white onions, peeled (can be frozen)

3 medium parsnips, peeled and cut into 3 to 4 chunks

1 1/2 pounds medium thin-skinned potatoes, scrubbed and quartered

2 tablespoons all-purpose flour mashed into 2 tablespoons unsalted butter at room temperature

Drizzle 1 tablespoon of the soy sauce onto a plate and roll the roast in it, adding more soy sauce, if needed, to thoroughly coat. Slice the garlic into very thin slivers and make incisions about 3/4 inch deep in spots evenly distributed around the roast. Push one sliver of garlic into each incision with your finger. Season the roast liberally with pepper.

Heat the oil in the cooker over medium-high heat. Sauté the chopped celery, carrot, and onion for 3 minutes, stirring occasionally; scrape up any browned bits sticking to the bottom of the pot. Add the beef broth (watch for sputtering oil), bay leaves, and thyme.

Immerse the rack or trivet into the liquid and place the meat on it, broad side down, so the most surface possible is submerged in the liquid.

Lock the lid in place and over high heat bring to high pressure. Adjust the heat to maintain high pressure and cook for 45 to 50 minutes. Let the pressure drop naturally, 10 to 15 minutes. Remove the lid, tilting it away from you to allow steam to escape.

If the pot roast is done, it should be tender enough to be pierced easily with a fork. If it is not sufficiently tender, lock the lid back into place and return to high pressure for another 5 minutes. Again, let the pressure drop naturally.

When the roast is fork-tender, transfer it to a platter or cutting board and let it rest for 10 minutes before slicing and arranging on a platter.

Meanwhile, remove the rack from the cooker. Place the small onions, chunked parsnips, and quartered potatoes into the pot. Lock the lid in place and over high heat return to high pressure. Adjust the heat to maintain high pressure and cook for 5 minutes. Reduce the pressure with a quick-release method. Remove the lid, tilting it away from you to allow steam to escape. With a slotted spoon, lift the vegetables from the gravy and arrange them around the meat. Set aside in a warm place or tent with aluminum foil.

To prepare the gravy: Spoon off any surface fat or degrease the liquid in a fat separator and return to the cooker. Over high heat, gradually whisk the flour-butter mixture into the gravy. Cook over medium-high heat until the gravy thickens, stirring constantly, 3 to 4 minutes. Remove the bay leaves and adjust the seasonings.

Either serve the gravy in a sauceboat, or pour it over the sliced pot roast and vegetables and serve immediately.

Beef Chili

The quintessential American stew, chili has inspired whole cookbooks, and the debate on whether to include beans rages on. As a great bean lover, I consider chili naked without them, but the success of this stew doesn't depend on them.

For a delicious vegetarian version, substitute 1 pound of cubed, firm tofu for the beef. Skip the browning stage and use vegetable instead of beef broth. Reduce the cooking time to 7 minutes.　　SERVES 6

(16–20 MINUTES UNDER HIGH PRESSURE, THEN 10 MINUTES
FOR NATURAL PRESSURE RELEASE)

2 to 3 tablespoons olive oil

2 pounds boneless chuck or round, cut into 1-inch cubes, trimmed
　　of excess fat

1 large garlic clove, minced

3 cups coarsely chopped onion

1 green bell pepper, seeded and cut into strips

1 jalapeño pepper, seeded and chopped, or a few shakes of crushed
　　red pepper flakes (optional)

1 teaspoon whole cumin seeds

1 teaspoon dried oregano

1 three-inch cinnamon stick, broken in two

2 bay leaves

1 1/2 to 2 tablespoons chili powder

1/8 teaspoon ground nutmeg

1 teaspoon salt, or to taste (less if using canned broth or bouillon)

One 28-ounce can tomatoes, coarsely chopped, including juice

1 to 2 cups cooked red kidney beans (optional)

1 cup tightly packed, minced fresh cilantro

2 tablespoons finely ground yellow cornmeal (optional)

Garnishes: grated Cheddar and finely chopped onions (optional)

Heat 2 tablespoons oil in the cooker. Over medium-high heat, brown the meat in two to three batches. Remove to a platter and set aside.

Adding more oil if necessary, sauté the garlic, onions, green pepper, and jalapeño pepper (if desired) for 3 minutes, scraping up any browned bits from the bottom of the pan. Return the browned meat to the pot. Stir in the spices and salt. Pour the tomatoes on top. *Do not stir.*

Lock the lid in place and over high heat bring to high pressure. Adjust the heat to maintain high pressure and cook for 16 minutes. Let the pressure drop naturally, about 10 minutes. *Do not use a quick-release method.* Remove the lid, tilting it away from you to allow steam to escape.

Test the beef for doneness. If it is not sufficiently tender, lock the lid back into place and return to high pressure for a few more minutes. Again, let the pressure drop naturally. When the beef is tender, remove the bay leaves and cinnamon sticks. Stir in the kidney beans (if using) and cilantro. If the chili is too thin, gradually whisk in the cornmeal while boiling over medium heat until thickened. Pass the Cheddar cheese and chopped onions on the side, if desired.

Porcupine Meatballs

When I mentioned work in progress on this cookbook, my Boston-based food colleague Joyce Toomre immediately replied, "Oh, you must make porcupine meatballs. We doctor up the recipe that's in the old Presto cookbook, and they've been a weekly standby in my family for years."

Sure enough, the recipe appears in all of the Presto cookbooks, old and current. The original version is quite simple, calling for ground beef, rice, salt, pepper, and a bit of minced onion. The meatballs are cooked in a small can of tomato soup concentrate.

Here's my gussied-up version. It may not sound very modest, but they are delicious, and kids (grown-ups, too) find it amusing to see the cooked rice sticking out all over the place.

To cook the rice properly, the meatballs must sit in a single layer directly in the liquid; make them in two separate batches if necessary. I sit the meatballs in water and pour the tomatoes on top to prevent scorching the bottom of the cooker as it comes up to pressure. Avoid using a tomato sauce that has bits of mushroom or sausage in it, as they have a tendency to sink and stick to the bottom of the cooker. SERVES 4–5

(5 MINUTES UNDER HIGH PRESSURE, THEN 7 MINUTES FOR
NATURAL PRESSURE RELEASE)

1 1/2 pounds ground beef or a combination of 3/4 pound ground beef
    and 3/4 pound ground pork
1/2 cup uncooked long-grain white rice
1/2 cup finely chopped onion
1 large garlic clove, minced
1/4 cup finely chopped fresh parsley
2 tablespoons coarsely chopped capers (optional)
1/2 teaspoon salt, or to taste
1 cup water
3 cups tomato sauce
1 tablespoon cornstarch
Garnish: grated Parmesan (optional)

In a large bowl, combine all the ingredients except the water, tomato sauce, and Parmesan. Roll into 17 or 18 meatballs, each about 2 inches in diameter.

Pour the water into the cooker. Set the meatballs side by side in the water; don't stack them on top of each other. (You may have to cook the meatballs in two batches.) Pour the tomato sauce on top. *Do not stir.*

Lock the lid in place and over high heat bring to high pressure. Adjust the heat to maintain high pressure and cook for 5 minutes. Let the pressure drop naturally, about 7 minutes. Remove the lid, tilting it away from you to allow steam to escape.

Check for doneness by splitting open a meatball and making sure that the rice on the inside is thoroughly cooked. If not, set the lid back in place and let the meatballs steam in the residual heat for a minute or two.

Lift the meatballs from the pot with a slotted spoon and set on a warm platter. If the sauce is too thin for your taste, boil vigorously over high heat until reduced to the desired consistency. Alternatively, blend the cornstarch into 1 tablespoon of water and stir it in. Cook over medium-high heat, stirring frequently until the sauce thickens.

Pour over the meatballs and serve, topped with grated Parmesan if desired.

Brisket with Sweet Potatoes and Prunes

This is an especially hearty version of the Jewish tsimmes. *It's best when made the day before and refrigerated so that the congealed fat can be easily removed from the gravy. Just before serving, the gravy is cooked with apple cider, prunes, sweet potatoes, and parsnips and poured over the sliced reheated meat.*

Don't be concerned if the brisket has to be squeezed against the sides of the pot; it will shrink considerably during cooking.　　SERVES 4–6

(55–65 MINUTES UNDER HIGH PRESSURE, THEN 10–15 MINUTES
FOR NATURAL PRESSURE RELEASE (BRISKET), THEN 3 MINUTES
UNDER HIGH PRESSURE (VEGETABLES))

2 to 3 tablespoons oil or chicken fat
3 1/2 pounds boneless beef brisket
2 celery stalks, finely chopped
2 large carrots, finely chopped
1 large onion, finely chopped
2 cups beef broth or bouillon
1 cup water
1 1/4 teaspoons ground cinnamon
1/4 teaspoon ground nutmeg
1/8 teaspoon ground allspice
1/2 to 1 cup apple cider
2 pounds sweet potatoes, peeled and cut into 1/2-inch slices
1 1/2 pounds parsnips, peeled and cut into 1-inch chunks
1 cup pitted prunes, coarsely chopped
Salt and freshly ground black pepper

Heat 2 tablespoons oil or chicken fat in the cooker. Over high heat, brown the meat well on both sides, lifting it up frequently with tongs or a spatula to prevent sticking. Add the additional tablespoon of oil, if needed. Set aside.

In the oil remaining in the cooker, sauté the chopped celery, carrots, and onion for 3 minutes, stirring occasionally. Add the beef broth (watch for sputtering oil), water, cinnamon, nutmeg, and allspice. Take care to scrape up any browned bits of meat or vegetables that are sticking to the bottom of the pot.

Submerge the rack or trivet into this mixture, and place the meat on it with the fat side facing up.

Lock the lid in place and over high heat bring to high pressure. Adjust the heat to maintain high pressure and cook for 55 minutes. Let the pressure drop naturally, 10 to 15 minutes. Remove the lid, tilting it away from you to allow steam to escape.

If the brisket is done, you should easily be able to pry a small chunk of meat from one end with a fork. If it is not sufficiently tender, lock the lid back into place and return to high pressure for another 5 to 10 minutes. Again, let the pressure drop naturally.

When done, remove the brisket from the pot. If time permits, cool to room temperature and refrigerate the brisket and gravy overnight in a covered container. Remove any congealed fat the next morning and return the gravy to the cooker before proceeding with the recipe. Alternatively, use a gravy separator to defat the liquid.

About 20 minutes before serving, stir enough cider into the gravy to equal a total of approximately 2 cups. Add the sweet potatoes, parsnips, and prunes. Lock the lid in place and over high heat bring to high pressure. Adjust the heat to maintain high pressure and cook for 3 minutes. Quick-release the pressure. Remove the lid, tilting it away from you to allow steam to escape. Add salt and pepper to taste.

Cut the brisket into slices on the diagonal, against the grain. Place the slices in the cooker and spoon the gravy and vegetables on top. Set (but do not lock) the cover in place. Cook over medium heat just until the meat is warmed throughout. Arrange the meat on a platter and surround with the vegetables. Pour the gravy on top or serve it in a sauceboat.

🍲 LAMB 🍲

Before writing this book, I was not a fan of lamb stews. But the pressure cooker turns out such moist, tender, and flavorful lamb dishes—and in such record time—that I have become a convert.

Boned lamb shoulder is the ideal cut to use for a stew. Nine times out of ten, 12 minutes will cook it to perfection. On occasion—particularly when the meat is from an older animal—you'll need to add another 3 to 5 minutes to the cooking time. Quick-releasing works fine with lamb, but I prefer to let the pressure drop naturally when I have the time. Leftovers freeze beautifully.

Lamb Stew with Two Peppers

This colorful dish is prepared in two stages: First, the lamb is cooked under pressure. Then the peppers are added and simmered just until crisp-tender.

SERVES 4

(12–17 MINUTES UNDER HIGH PRESSURE,
THEN 5–8 MINUTES SIMMERING)

2 pounds boned lamb shoulder, trimmed and cut into 2-inch cubes
Salt and freshly ground black pepper
2 tablespoons olive oil
2 medium onions, thinly sliced
3 large garlic cloves, minced
2 tablespoons tomato paste
1/4 cup red wine vinegar, preferably balsamic
1/2 cup water
2 teaspoons sweet paprika, preferably Spanish or Hungarian
1 1/2 teaspoons dried thyme
2 bay leaves
One 14-ounce can diced tomatoes, including juice
1 large red bell pepper, seeded and cut into eighths
1 large green bell pepper, seeded and cut into eighths

Season the lamb well with salt and pepper to taste. Set aside.

Heat the oil in the cooker. Sauté the onions and garlic until the onions are soft, about 3 minutes. Stir in the tomato paste and cook an additional minute.

Stir in the vinegar and, while cooking for a minute or two over medium-high heat, scrape up any browned bits stuck to the bottom of the cooker.

Stir in the water, paprika, thyme, and bay leaves. Add the lamb. Pour the tomatoes on top. *Do not stir.*

Lock the lid in place and over high heat bring to high pressure. Adjust the heat to maintain high pressure and cook for 12 minutes. Let the

pressure drop naturally, 7 to 10 minutes, or use a quick-release method. Remove the lid, tilting it away from you to allow steam to escape.

Remove the bay leaves, and stir in the peppers. Cover and simmer over medium heat until the peppers are crisp-tender, another 5 to 8 minutes. Adjust the seasonings before serving.

Moroccan Lamb Tagine

This dish was inspired by the evocative tastes and aromas in Paula Wolfert's classic **Couscous and Other Good Food from Morocco** *(Harper & Row, 1973). "Nowadays, everyone in Morocco is cooking their tagines in pressure cookers," commented Paula when she heard I was writing this book. Serve the tagine with couscous or Fragrant Coconut Rice (page 220).* SERVES 4–6

(12–17 MINUTES UNDER HIGH PRESSURE)

1 tablespoon olive oil

1 large onion, coarsely chopped

2^1/$_2$ pounds boned lamb shoulder, trimmed and cut into 2-inch cubes

1 cup water

3 large carrots, peeled (leave whole)

1 cup tightly packed pitted prunes (about 20)

1 large lemon, cut into 8 wedges and seeded

1/2 teaspoon ground cinnamon

1 teaspoon ground ginger

1 teaspoon salt, or to taste

1/2 cup coarsely chopped fresh cilantro

Garnish: 1/2 cup toasted blanched almonds (optional)

Heat the oil and sauté the onion until lightly browned, 4 to 5 minutes. Stir in the remaining ingredients except for the cilantro and almonds.

Lock the lid in place and over high heat bring to high pressure. Adjust the heat to maintain high pressure and cook for 12 minutes. Let the pressure drop naturally or use a quick-release method. Remove the lid, tilting it away from you to allow steam to escape.

Slash the carrots with a knife. Stir in the cilantro. Adjust the seasonings and transfer to a serving platter. Garnish with toasted almonds, if desired.

Lamb with Olives

With its thin, flavor-packed broth, this zesty stew is best served in bowls over noodles, couscous, or rice. Olives and lamb bring out the best in each other. SERVES 6

(12–17 MINUTES UNDER HIGH PRESSURE)

1 tablespoon olive oil
2 garlic cloves, minced
1 large onion, halved and cut into 1/2-inch slices
2 1/2 pounds boned lamb shoulder, trimmed and cut into 2-inch cubes
4 medium thin-skinned potatoes, scrubbed and quartered
2 large carrots, peeled (leave whole)
1 cup pimiento-stuffed olives, divided
1/2 cup beef broth or bouillon
1/2 cup dry red wine or additional broth
1 teaspoon ground ginger
1/2 teaspoon *each* ground cinnamon, cumin, and cardamom
1/2 teaspoon *each* ground turmeric and crushed red pepper flakes
Salt and freshly ground black pepper
1/3 cup minced fresh cilantro
Juice of 1/2 large lemon

Heat the oil in the cooker. Sauté the garlic and onion until the onion is lightly browned, stirring occasionally, about 3 minutes. Add the lamb, potatoes, carrots, half the olives, the broth, wine, spices, and salt and pepper to taste.

Lock the lid in place and over high heat bring to high pressure. Adjust the heat to maintain high pressure and cook for 12 minutes. Let the pressure drop naturally, 7 to 10 minutes, or use a quick-release method. Remove the lid, tilting it away from you to allow steam to escape.

Slash the carrots with a knife. Stir in the cilantro, lemon juice, and remaining olives. Adjust the seasonings and serve.

Lamb Curry

A delicious curry made with dried coconut, this dish is great with a simple rice pilaf and your favorite chutney. Curried Cauliflower and Potatoes (page 142) also work well as an accompaniment.

This recipe produces a rich sauce, which can be served with the curry; you can thicken it by stirring in about 1/3 cup of finely ground almonds while simmering over medium heat. If you prefer a drier curry, drain off the liquid and reserve it for another use, such as broth for cooking rice or other grains. Then cook the lamb over medium-high heat for a few minutes, stirring constantly, until any remaining liquid evaporates.

SERVES 4

(12–17 MINUTES UNDER HIGH PRESSURE)

1 tablespoon oil

2 cups coarsely chopped onions

2 teaspoons finely minced garlic

1 tablespoon finely minced ginger

2 cups water

1 cup unsweetened flaked or grated coconut (available in health-food stores)

2 1/2 pounds boned lamb shoulder, trimmed and cut into 2-inch cubes

2 large carrots, scrubbed and coarsely chopped

1/2 cup raisins, preferably golden

1 tablespoon plus 2 teaspoons mild curry powder

1/8 teaspoon cayenne pepper, or to taste

1 teaspoon salt, or to taste

Garnish: 1/3 cup finely chopped fresh cilantro (optional)

Heat the oil in the cooker. Sauté the onions and garlic until the onions are soft, about 3 minutes. Stir in the remaining ingredients except the cilantro. Lock the lid in place and over high heat bring to high pressure. Adjust the heat to maintain high pressure and cook for 12 minutes. Let the pressure drop naturally or use a quick-release method. Remove the lid, tilting it away from you to allow steam to escape.

Drain off the liquid, if you wish. Adjust the seasonings and garnish the lamb with chopped cilantro, if desired.

☕ VEAL ☕

Here are recipes for veal in three very different guises. Veal Paprika is one of those dishes you just can't stop eating, and the creamy Blanquette de Veau brings a taste of the French country kitchen to your home. Perhaps the award for the greatest pressure-cooker triumph in this category goes to Pat Baird's Osso Buco, a preparation of braised Italian veal shanks that most people leave to the know-how of restaurant chefs. "A marvelous dish," commented the friend who retested it for me while I was working on this book. "I want the recipe back as soon as possible—*please.*"

Veal Paprika

A rich and filling dish traditionally served over wide egg noodles. For best results, use imported sweet paprika (available in gourmet shops) rather than supermarket brands, which tend to be rather bland.

SERVES 6

(10 MINUTES UNDER HIGH PRESSURE)

2¹/₂ to 3 pounds boned veal shoulder, trimmed and cut into
   2-inch cubes
3 to 4 tablespoons all-purpose flour
2 tablespoons oil
1 cup chicken broth or bouillon
1 garlic clove, minced
2 medium onions, coarsely chopped
1 tablespoon sweet paprika, preferably Spanish or Hungarian
1 bay leaf
1 teaspoon dried thyme
1 tablespoon tomato paste
¹/₂ teaspoon salt, or to taste (less if using canned broth or bouillon)
Freshly ground black pepper
1 cup sour cream (low-fat is fine)
¹/₄ cup minced fresh parsley

Rinse the veal, pat dry, and dredge in flour, pressing the flour into the veal with the heel of your hand. Shake off extra flour.

Heat the oil in the cooker. Over medium heat, brown the veal on all sides in two to three batches. Remove the browned veal and set aside on a platter.

Add the broth and take care to scrape up any flour stuck to the bottom of the cooker. Stir in the garlic, onions, paprika, bay leaf, thyme, tomato paste, and salt and pepper to taste. Add the browned veal, including any juices that have collected in the platter.

Lock the lid in place and over high heat bring to high pressure. Adjust the heat to maintain high pressure and cook for 10 minutes. Let the

pressure drop naturally or use a quick-release method. Remove the lid, tilting it away from you to allow steam to escape.

Remove the bay leaf. Stir about $1/2$ cup of the gravy into the sour cream. Then stir this mixture and the parsley into the pot. Adjust the seasonings before serving.

Pat Baird's Osso Buco

My colleague Pat Baird has been in quest of the perfect osso buco for years; she may well have found it with this version. This classic dish cooks to perfection in the pressure cooker. After the shanks are done, a delicious garlic-parsley paste called gremolata *is stirred in, adding a fresh and flavorful finish.*

Serve with a simple risotto, orzo, or thin spaghetti to drink up the garlicky sauce. SERVES 4

(18 MINUTES UNDER HIGH PRESSURE)

4 veal shanks, about 10 ounces each (see Note)
2 tablespoons all-purpose flour
3 tablespoons olive oil, divided
3/4 cup dry red wine or dry vermouth
1 large onion, coarsely chopped
2 medium carrots, coarsely chopped
1 celery stalk, sliced
1/2 pound mushrooms, sliced
1 teaspoon dried basil
1 teaspoon dried oregano
1/2 teaspoon salt, or to taste
Freshly ground black pepper
One 15-ounce can diced tomatoes, including juice

FOR THE GREMOLATA
1 tablespoon finely minced garlic
2 tablespoons grated lemon zest
1/2 cup finely minced fresh parsley

Rinse the veal shanks, pat dry, and dredge in flour, pressing the flour into the veal with the heel of your hand. Shake off extra flour.

Heat 2 tablespoons oil in the cooker. Over medium heat, brown the veal on both sides and set aside on a platter.

Add the red wine and stir, taking care to scrape up any browned bits that are stuck to the bottom of the pan. Add the onions, carrots, celery, mushrooms, basil, oregano, and salt and pepper to taste. Add the shanks and pour the tomatoes on top. *Do not stir.*

Lock the lid in place and over high heat bring to high pressure. Adjust the heat to maintain high pressure and cook for 18 minutes. Let the pressure drop naturally or use a quick-release method. Remove the lid, tilting it away from you to allow steam to escape.

Prepare the *gremolata* by combining the garlic, lemon zest, and parsley. When the shanks are done, stir in the *gremolata* and simmer for a few minutes. Adjust the seasonings and serve.

NOTE: If using smaller shanks, check for doneness after 15 minutes under high pressure.

Blanquette de Veau

This is French home cooking at its finest. Although it is traditionally made with the economical breast of veal (which has a uniquely chewy texture), you might prefer the more tender shoulder cut. The traditional version is thickened with egg yolks and enriched with heavy cream; I've cut the fat by thickening with the classic beurre manié: flour rubbed into butter. Serve the blanquette *in soup plates over egg noodles or rice—wild rice is especially good.*

SERVES 6

(10–15 MINUTES UNDER HIGH PRESSURE)

2 1/2 pounds boned veal shoulder or breast, trimmed and cut into
    1-inch cubes
1 cup chicken broth or bouillon
1/2 cup dry white wine or vermouth
Bunch of parsley stems, tied with a string
1 bay leaf
1 teaspoon minced garlic
Large pinch of ground allspice
3/4 pound (8 to 10) small white onions, peeled (frozen are fine)
1/2 pound mushrooms, quartered
2 tablespoons all-purpose flour mashed into 2 tablespoons
    unsalted butter, at room temperature
1/2 teaspoon salt, or to taste (less if using canned broth or bouillon)
Freshly ground white pepper
1 1/2 cups frozen peas (optional)

Combine the veal, broth, wine, parsley, bay leaf, garlic, allspice, onions, and mushrooms in the cooker.

Lock the lid in place and over high heat bring to high pressure. Adjust the heat to maintain high pressure and cook for 10 minutes if using veal shoulder, or 15 minutes if using breast of veal. Let the pressure drop naturally or use a quick-release method. Remove the lid, tilting it away from you to allow steam to escape.

Remove the parsley sprigs and bay leaf. If the sauce is fatty, either spoon off the surface fat or use a gravy separator. While maintaining the sauce at a gentle boil, slowly whisk in bits of the flour-butter mixture. Add salt and pepper to taste. Continue to cook until the sauce is thick enough to lightly coat the back of a spoon and the flour tastes cooked, about 5 minutes. Toward the end of cooking, stir in the peas (if using) and cook only until they defrost and are still bright green, about 1 minute.

PORK AND HAM

Pork cooks very quickly under pressure and the tougher cuts like shoulder and ribs take beautifully to moist cooking. Like chicken, pork marries well with a wide variety of flavors—a fact I have taken full advantage of in the recipes that follow.

Pork Braised in Beer and Onions

Based on the Flemish carbonnade, *this recipe relies upon the complex flavor of beer to create a full-flavored meat and gravy. The spices rubbed directly on the pork shoulder enhance the flavor of the meat. For a quicker-cooking dish, cut the pork shoulder into 1-inch cubes (or purchase already cubed pork), and reduce the cooking time to 8 minutes!*

The abundant gravy is thickened, then poured over the carved pork. Great over wide noodles or dumplings.   SERVES 6

(45–50 MINUTES UNDER HIGH PRESSURE)

2 teaspoons minced garlic

1 tablespoon soy sauce

2 packed tablespoons brown sugar

1/4 teaspoon ground allspice

1/4 teaspoon cayenne pepper

1/2 teaspoon salt, or to taste

3 1/2 to 4 pounds (trimmed weight) picnic shoulder, rind removed

1 cup beer

2 bay leaves

6 cups tightly packed, sliced onion

2 tablespoons cornstarch dissolved in 2 tablespoons water

In a small bowl, make a paste by mashing together the garlic, soy sauce, sugar, allspice, cayenne, and salt. Rub into the picnic shoulder.

Add half of the onions. Pour the beer into the cooker and add the bay leaves. Set the rack on top of the onions, and set the pork on top of the rack. Spread the remaining onions over the pork.

Lock the lid in place and over high heat bring to high pressure. Adjust the heat to maintain high pressure and cook for 55 minutes. Let the pressure drop naturally or use a quick-release method. Remove the lid, tilting it away from you to allow steam to escape.

Check the pork for doneness with a meat thermometer inserted into the center. It should register 170 degrees Fahrenheit. If not, lock the lid back in place and return the pork to high pressure for a few more minutes. Remove the pork to a cutting board and let rest for 5 to 10 minutes. Remove the rack from the cooker.

If there is more than about 2 cups of sauce, boil vigorously over high heat to reduce. Whisk in the cornstarch solution to thicken the gravy while cooking at a low boil for 2 to 3 minutes. Remove the bay leaves and adjust the seasonings.

To serve, carve the pork and set on a platter. Pour the gravy on top or serve on the side in a sauceboat.

Mexican-Style Pork Stew

This wonderfully seasoned stew is the creation of my colleague Stephen Schmidt (a.k.a. Señor Picante), author of the masterful and encyclopedic teaching cookbook Master Recipes.

Keep in mind that two chile peppers make the dish quite hot; eight make it fire-department material. Wash it all down with ice-cold beer.

SERVES 4–6

(8 MINUTES UNDER HIGH PRESSURE)

1 tablespoon olive oil

1 cup coarsely chopped onions

1 cup chicken broth or bouillon

2 teaspoons ground cinnamon

1 teaspoon dried oregano

1/4 teaspoon ground cloves

1/2 teaspoon salt, or to taste (less if using canned broth or bouillon)

1/4 teaspoon freshly ground black pepper

1/2 cup pitted prunes

21/2 pounds pork shoulder, neck, or arm, trimmed and cut into
    11/2-inch cubes

One 14-ounce can tomatoes, coarsely chopped, including juice

1 cup sliced pimiento-stuffed green olives

1 cup chopped fresh or drained canned, crushed pineapple

2 jalapeño or other fresh chile peppers, seeded and cut into thin
    strips (see Note)

2 garlic cloves, peeled

1 tablespoon cornstarch (optional)

Heat the oil in the cooker. Over medium-high heat, cook the onions until lightly browned, about 3 minutes. Add the broth, cinnamon, oregano, cloves, salt, pepper, prunes, and pork shoulder. Pour the tomatoes on top. *Do not stir.*

Lock the lid in place and over high heat bring to high pressure. Adjust the heat to maintain high pressure and cook for 8 minutes. Let the

pressure drop naturally. Remove the lid, tilting it away from you to allow steam to escape.

Stir in the olives, pineapple, and jalapeños. Push the garlic cloves through a press and stir in.

Thicken the sauce, if desired, by blending the cornstarch into 1 tablespoon of water. Stir this mixture into the stew and cook at the gentle boil, stirring frequently, until thickened, 3 to 5 minutes.

NOTE: When working with fresh chile peppers, either wear rubber gloves or wash your hands thoroughly after touching them. If fresh chile peppers are unavailable, substitute all or part of a 4-ounce can, thoroughly drained and chopped. Then season the stew with cayenne pepper to taste to compensate for the relative blandness of the canned chiles.

Pork Chops with Sausage and Sauerkraut

Here is a simplified and very tasty version of the famous Alsatian chou-croute garni. *Serve it with German or French mustard and a cold beer.*

SERVES 4

(10 MINUTES UNDER HIGH PRESSURE)

2 pounds fresh (refrigerated) sauerkraut

1 to 3 tablespoons oil

1/2 pound kielbasa or other smoked pork sausage, casings removed
    if necessary, cut into 1/2-inch slices

4 pork shoulder chops, approximately 1 inch thick, trimmed of
    excess fat

1 large onion, coarsely chopped

4 large garlic cloves, peeled and left whole

1 cup chicken broth or bouillon

1/3 cup loosely packed dried mushrooms (1/2 ounce)

1 bay leaf

1 tablespoon caraway seeds

5 juniper berries (optional)

6 whole black peppercorns

6 whole cloves

1 1/4 pounds (about 10) small new potatoes

1/4 teaspoon salt, or to taste

Place the sauerkraut in a colander and rinse it thoroughly to remove some of the salt. (If the sauerkraut is quite salty, soak it for 5 to 10 minutes in two changes of water.) Set aside to drain.

Heat 1 tablespoon of the oil in the cooker and brown the sausage slices well on both sides. Set aside. Brown the pork chops, two at a time, adding more oil if needed. Set aside.

Sauté the onions and garlic until the onions are light brown, about 3 minutes. Stir in the broth, mushrooms, bay leaf, caraway seeds, juniper berries (if using), peppercorns, and cloves, taking care to scrape up any browned bits that are sticking to the bottom of the cooker.

Place half of the sauerkraut onto this mixture and lay the pork chops on top. Place the remaining sauerkraut on top of the chops. Set the potatoes on the sauerkraut and sprinkle lightly with salt.

Lock the lid in place and over high heat bring to high pressure. Adjust the heat to maintain high pressure and cook for 10 minutes. Reduce the pressure with a quick-release method. Remove the lid, tilting it away from you to allow steam to escape.

Remove the bay leaf and adjust the seasonings. Set the potatoes around the edges of a platter. Lift the pork chops and sauerkraut with a slotted spoon and set them in the center of the platter. Stir in the browned kielbasa to heat it. If you wish to thicken the gravy, puree a few of the potatoes and stir them into the gravy. Pour some of the gravy on the sauerkraut and serve the rest in a sauceboat.

Pork and Bean Casserole with Sausage and Lamb

Inspired by the famous Southwest French cassoulet, *this aromatic stew develops a flavorful, creamy sauce with the addition of cooked beans. The sauce may seem thin at first, but it thickens considerably after overnight refrigeration or a few hours of standing at room temperature. If you're serving immediately and want a thicker sauce, lift out some of the beans with a slotted spoon, puree them, and stir them back into the stew.*

SERVES 6–8

(12–15 MINUTES UNDER HIGH PRESSURE)

1 tablespoon olive oil

1 pound cured garlic sausage, casings removed if necessary, cut into 1-inch slices

2 cups coarsely chopped leeks (white part only) or onions

3 large garlic cloves, minced

1 cup beef broth or bouillon

1 pound boned pork shoulder, trimmed and cut into 2-inch cubes

1$1/2$ pounds boned lamb shoulder, trimmed and cut into 1$1/2$-inch cubes

4 to 5 cups cooked Great Northern or navy beans

1 smoked ham hock

$1/3$ cup loosely packed dried mushrooms ($1/2$ ounce)

2 bay leaves

10 whole cloves

1 teaspoon dried thyme

1 teaspoon dried oregano

3 large carrots, peeled (leave whole)

One 14-ounce can tomatoes, coarsely chopped, including juice

$1/4$ cup finely minced fresh parsley

Salt and freshly ground black pepper

Heat the oil in the cooker and brown the sausage slices on both sides. Set aside. Add the leeks and garlic and cook over medium-high heat until the leeks begin to soften, about 3 minutes. Add the broth, taking care to scrape up any browned bits stuck to the bottom of the cooker. Stir in half of the sausage, the pork, lamb, beans, ham hock, mushrooms, bay leaves, cloves, thyme, and oregano. Set the carrots on top. Pour the tomatoes on top. *Do not stir.*

Lock the lid in place and over high heat bring to high pressure. Adjust the heat to maintain high pressure and cook for 12 minutes. Let the pressure drop naturally or use a quick-release method. Remove the lid, tilting it away from you to allow steam to escape.

Remove and discard the ham hock and bay leaves. Coarsely chop the remaining sausage and stir it in along with the parsley. Add salt and pepper to taste.

"Barbecued" Spareribs

If you love spareribs but are skeptical about the success of preparing them anywhere besides a grill, give this recipe a try. These ribs have a real barbecued flavor. Add some Tabasco or chile peppers for a sauce that's fiery hot. Or substitute your favorite barbecue sauce for the homemade version.

You can also finish off the ribs on a grill—skip the browning and cook in the sauce as directed, then grill for 2 to 3 minutes on each side, basting frequently with additional sauce—or set the cooked ribs under a broiler to achieve a crispy crust. SERVES 6

(12–14 MINUTES UNDER HIGH PRESSURE)

2 to 3 tablespoons oil

5 pounds spareribs, cut into serving pieces (about 3 to 4 ribs each)

1 cup water

1 green bell pepper, seeded and diced

1 cup coarsely chopped onion

1 cup catsup

2/3 cup cider vinegar

1/4 cup soy sauce

1/2 cup dry sherry

1 tablespoon dry mustard

2 tablespoons brown sugar

1 tablespoon minced garlic

1/2 teaspoon salt, or to taste

3/4 teaspoon freshly ground black pepper

Heat 1 tablespoon of the oil in the cooker. Over high heat, brown the spareribs well in several batches, removing them to a platter when done. Add more oil as needed. (Use a large skillet in addition to the cooker to speed up this process.)

Tip off or sop up any excess fat. Add the water and scrape up any browned bits sticking to the bottom of the cooker. Add the green pepper and onion and set the browned ribs on top.

In a bowl, combine the remaining ingredients for the sauce. Pour the sauce over the ribs. *Do not stir.*

Lock the lid in place and over high heat bring to high pressure. Adjust the heat to maintain high pressure and cook for 12 minutes. Reduce the pressure with a quick-release method. Remove the lid, tilting it away from you to allow steam to escape.

Check the pork for doneness by seeing if the meat can easily be separated from the bone when poked with a fork.

Transfer the ribs to a serving platter. If the sauce is too thin, boil it vigorously over high heat until it reaches a glazing consistency. Adjust the seasonings and pour over the ribs. Serve immediately.

Ham and Melted Cheese "Pudding"

This unusual dish is a cross between a melted cheese sandwich and a quiche. It's a quick and easy lunch, and a great use for leftover ham and day-old bread.

When you scoop out your first portion, you may find some liquid on the bottom of the dish. Just tip it off, or use a slotted spoon to serve the remaining portions. The taste will not be affected.　　SERVES 4

(15 MINUTES UNDER HIGH PRESSURE, THEN 10 MINUTES FOR NATURAL PRESSURE RELEASE)

1 to 2 tablespoons unsalted butter, plus butter for greasing the soufflé dish

8 to 9 1/2-inch-thick slices whole wheat or white Italian or French bread, left out overnight to dry

1 cup milk

5 large eggs, lightly beaten

1 tablespoon mustard, preferably Dijon

1/2 cup finely minced fresh parsley

1 1/4 cups grated Gruyère

1 cup diced, cooked country ham

1 cup thinly sliced scallions

Generously butter a 5-cup soufflé dish or suitable alternative. Cut a piece of aluminum foil about 1 foot wide and 2 feet long and fold it twice lengthwise to create a long strip for lowering the pudding into the cooker. Set aside.

Butter the bread and cut each slice into 2 to 3 pieces. Arrange one-third of the bread on the bottom of the soufflé dish.

In a bowl, combine the milk, eggs, and mustard and pour one-third of this mixture over the bread, turning the pieces so that they thoroughly absorb the liquid. Distribute one-third of the parsley, Gruyère, ham, and scallions on top. Repeat layering bread, liquid, parsley, Gruyère, ham, and scallions in this manner two more times, reserving some parsley and scallions for the top.

Cover the dish with aluminum foil so that the foil fits tightly around the sides, but allow some room on top for the pudding to expand.

Set a trivet or steaming rack on the bottom of the cooker. Center the pudding dish on the aluminum foil strip and gently lower the pudding onto the rack. Loosely fold the ends of the foil strip over the top of the dish. Pour enough water into the bottom of the pot to reach one-third up the sides of the soufflé dish.

Lock the lid in place and over high heat bring to high pressure. Adjust the heat to maintain high pressure and cook for 15 minutes. Let the pressure drop naturally, about 10 minutes. Remove the lid, tilting it away from you to allow steam to escape.

Let the pudding cool slightly before lifting it from the cooker with the aid of the aluminum foil strip. If you are not serving the pudding immediately, cut a few slits in the foil top and let it remain warm in the cooker, placing the lid slightly ajar for up to 1 hour.

To serve, scoop out portions with a large spoon.

An Unconventional Jambalaya

I couldn't resist preparing a New Orleans–style jambalaya with short-grain brown rice instead of the traditional white rice. Brown rice has a full-bodied flavor that stands up well to the spicy sausage, and the short-grain variety has a chewy texture that makes it resistant to overcooking.

SERVES 4

(15 MINUTES UNDER HIGH PRESSURE, THEN 10 MINUTES FOR NATURAL PRESSURE RELEASE)

2 tablespoons olive oil

3 large garlic cloves, minced

2 cups coarsely chopped onion

1/2 pound garlic sausage, casings removed if necessary, cut into 1/2-inch slices (see Note)

1 1/4 cups uncooked short- or long-grain brown rice

1/2 pound cooked country ham, cut into 1/2-inch cubes

4 celery stalks, cut into 1/2-inch slices

1 large green bell pepper, seeded and cut into 1-inch strips

2 cups water

1 bay leaf

2 tablespoons tomato paste

1/2 teaspoon salt, or to taste

Tabasco or cayenne pepper

1/2 cup tightly packed, minced fresh cilantro

Heat the oil in the cooker. Sauté the garlic and onion for 3 minutes. Push the onion and garlic aside, and brown the sausage slices about 30 seconds on each side. Stir in the rice, coating the grains with the fat. Add the ham, celery, green pepper, water, bay leaf, tomato paste, and salt and Tabasco to taste. Take care to scrape up any browned bits sticking to the bottom of the cooker.

Lock the lid in place and over high heat bring to high pressure. Adjust the heat to maintain high pressure and cook for 15 minutes. Let the pressure drop naturally for 10 minutes, then quick-release any remaining pressure. Remove the lid, tilting it away from you to allow steam to escape.

If the rice is slightly undercooked, cover and simmer over low heat for another 2 to 3 minutes; stir in a few tablespoons of water if the mixture is dry. Stir in the cilantro, adjust the seasonings, and serve.

NOTE: If the sausage is thick, cut the slices into 2 to 3 pieces.

CHICKEN

It's a breeze to prepare chicken in the pressure cooker. Young broilers are done to perfection in 9 minutes using a quick-release method, emerging from the pot tender and infused with flavor. (If you let the pressure drop naturally, reduce the cooking time under high pressure to 5 minutes.)

These recipes were all tested with young chicken parts. Pieces of an old stewing chicken are likely to require a bit more cooking than a young broiler, but always check for doneness after 9 minutes. If the chicken needs more cooking, lock the lid back in place and return to high pressure for a few minutes, or simmer over medium heat, partially covered, until done.

Thighs and drumsticks take especially well to this type of moist cooking, so don't hesitate to use them instead of the parts of a whole chicken. I recommend skinning chicken before cooking: Under pressure, the skin becomes loose and shriveled.

Coq au Vin

This is bistro food at its very best. Serve with rice, noodles, or boiled potatoes to absorb the flavorful sauce.

SERVES 4–6

(9–11 MINUTES UNDER HIGH PRESSURE, THEN 3–5 MINUTES SIMMERING)

3 to 4 slices bacon (about 2 ounces)

One 3$1/2$- to 4-pound chicken, cut into 8 pieces, skinned

1 to 2 tablespoons olive oil (optional)

3 medium leeks, white part only, thoroughly rinsed and thinly sliced (about 2 cups)

1 to 2 garlic cloves, finely minced

2 celery stalks, cut into $1/4$-inch slices

1 cup dry red wine

1 cup chicken broth or bouillon

1 bay leaf

1 teaspoon dried thyme

$1/2$ cup loosely packed dried mushrooms ($1/3$ ounce)

1 pound (about 12) small white onions (frozen is fine)

$1/4$ cup finely minced fresh parsley

2 tablespoons all-purpose flour mashed into 2 tablespoons unsalted butter at room temperature

Salt and freshly ground black pepper

Over medium heat, fry the bacon in the cooker to render the fat and become crisp. Remove the bacon and set aside. In the bacon fat, brown the chicken, 3 to 4 pieces at a time, adding oil if needed. Set the chicken aside.

Add more oil if needed, and sauté the leeks and garlic until the leeks are soft, stirring frequently, 2 to 3 minutes. Stir in the celery and red wine, using a spoon to scrape up any browned bits stuck to the bottom of the pot. Cook until most of the wine evaporates, about 2 minutes. Stir in the broth, bay leaf, thyme, dried mushrooms, and onions. Return the chicken to the pot.

Lock the lid in place and over high heat bring to high pressure. Adjust the heat to maintain high pressure and cook for 9 minutes. Reduce the pressure with a quick-release method. Remove the lid, tilting it away from you to allow steam to escape.

Lift the chicken and onions with a slotted spoon and set into a hot casserole or deep serving platter. Tent with aluminum foil to keep warm.

Discard the bay leaf. Boil the sauce over medium heat, stir in the parsley, then gradually whisk in the butter-flour mixture. Add salt and pepper to taste. Cook, stirring constantly, until the sauce thickens and the flour tastes cooked, 3 to 5 minutes. Pour the sauce over the chicken and crumble the crisped bacon on top before serving.

Chicken with Lentils and Spinach

A colorful soupy stew—spinach green and carrot orange—that reverberates with the tastes of faraway places. If you like, use a 12-ounce bag of fresh baby spinach instead of frozen spinach.

A neighbor who tasted some asked to borrow a pressure cooker and proceeded to make this recipe four nights in a row.

Serve with rice or couscous and a bottle of harissa on the side.

SERVES 4–6

(9–11 MINUTES UNDER HIGH PRESSURE, THEN 2 MINUTES SIMMERING)

2 tablespoons olive oil
1 large onion, coarsely chopped
1 tablespoon whole cumin seeds
1 1/2 cups dried lentils, picked over and rinsed
2 to 2 1/2 pounds chicken parts (dark meat remains moister), skinned
3 1/2 cups water
1/4 teaspoon ground allspice
1/2 teaspoon ground cinnamon
2/3 cup raisins
2 large carrots, peeled (leave whole)
One 10-ounce package frozen leaf spinach, defrosted
1 to 2 teaspoons finely minced fresh ginger
1 teaspoon salt, or to taste

Heat the oil in the cooker. Sauté the onion until lightly browned, stirring frequently, 3 to 4 minutes. Stir in the cumin seeds and sauté an additional 10 seconds. Add the lentils, chicken, carrots, water, allspice, cinnamon, and raisins. Stir to scrape up any browned bits sticking to the bottom of the cooker. Set the carrots on top.

Lock the lid in place and over high heat bring to high pressure.

Adjust the heat to maintain high pressure and cook for 9 minutes. Reduce the pressure with a quick-release method. Remove the lid, tilting it away from you to allow steam to escape.

Slash the carrots with a knife. Stir in the spinach and ginger. Add salt to taste. Simmer until the spinach is cooked, about 2 minutes.

Chicken Cacciatore

If you can, prepare this hearty stew the day before and refrigerate overnight. The flavors will keep getting richer and richer. There's lots of sauce, so plan to serve the cacciatore over orzo, noodles, spaghetti, or rice.

SERVES 4

(9–11 MINUTES UNDER HIGH PRESSURE)

2 to 3 tablespoons olive oil

1 large onion, coarsely chopped

1 large green bell pepper, seeded and coarsely chopped

2 celery stalks, thinly sliced

2/3 cup dry white wine

1/2 pound mushrooms, quartered or sliced

2 bay leaves

Generous pinch of crushed red pepper flakes (optional)

1 teaspoon dried oregano

1 teaspoon fennel seeds

1/2 teaspoon dried thyme or dried marjoram

1 teaspoon salt, or to taste

Freshly ground black pepper

One 3- to 3 1/2-pound chicken, cut into 8 pieces, skinned

One 28-ounce can tomatoes, coarsely chopped, including juice

1/4 cup finely minced fresh parsley

2 large garlic cloves, peeled

Heat 2 tablespoons olive oil in the cooker. Sauté the onion for 2 to 3 minutes. Stir in the green pepper and celery, and cook for another minute or two. Add the wine, stirring to scrape up any browned bits sticking to the bottom of the cooker.

Stir in the mushrooms, bay leaves, red pepper flakes (if desired), oregano, fennel, thyme, salt, and pepper to taste. Add the chicken. Pour the tomatoes on top. *Do not stir.*

Lock the lid in place and over high heat bring to high pressure. Adjust the heat to maintain high pressure and cook for 9 minutes. Reduce the pressure with a quick-release method. Remove the lid, tilting it away from you to allow steam to escape.

Remove the bay leaves and stir in the parsley. Pass the garlic cloves through a garlic press. Simmer until the garlic looses its raw taste and the chicken is thoroughly cooked, about 3 minutes. Adjust the seasonings before serving.

Chicken Curry

Irmgard Hamid, a member of my swim club, upon overhearing that I was writing this cookbook, jumped in and volunteered this "locker room" recipe. She was justly proud of the dish, perfected over the last two decades in her vintage pressure cooker.

This zesty curry is guaranteed to appeal to those who appreciate intense and complex flavors. Thoroughly browning the onions is necessary for best results. I often use only drumsticks and thighs, since dark meat stands up particularly well to the curry's flavor.

Serve with white or brown rice to absorb the plentiful, deep red sauce. Brown basmati rice is especially nice. SERVES 4–6

(9–11 MINUTES UNDER HIGH PRESSURE)

1 to 2 tablespoons oil

2 large onions, coarsely chopped

2 garlic cloves, finely minced

3 tablespoons tomato paste

1 teaspoon whole cumin seeds

1 tablespoon mild curry powder

$1/2$ teaspoon ground cinnamon

$1/2$ teaspoon ground cardamom

Generous pinch of cayenne pepper (optional)

1 cup chicken broth or bouillon

$1/2$ teaspoon salt, or to taste (less if using canned broth or bouillon)

$31/2$ to 4 pounds chicken parts, skinned

$11/2$ cups plain (unflavored) yogurt

1 to 2 tablespoons mango chutney

1–$11/2$ teaspoons finely minced fresh ginger

3 tablespoons chopped fresh cilantro (optional)

In a skillet, heat 1 tablespoon oil. Over medium heat, sauté the onions and garlic, stirring frequently, until the onions are very browned, 10 to 15 minutes. Add the additional tablespoon of oil, if needed. Stir in the tomato paste, cumin seeds, curry powder, and spices, and cook while stirring for 30 to 60 seconds, taking care to avoid burning.

Stir in the broth and salt. Scrape up any browned bits stuck to the bottom of the cooker. Add the chicken pieces.

Lock the lid in place and over high heat bring to high pressure. Adjust the heat to maintain high pressure and cook for 9 minutes. Reduce the pressure with a quick-release method.

While the chicken is cooking, blend 1 cup of yogurt with mango chutney and ginger to taste. When the chicken is done, ladle out about $^1/_2$ cup of the liquid and stir it into the remaining $^1/_2$ cup of yogurt. Stir this mixture into the pot. Adjust the seasonings.

To serve, spoon the curry over the rice and set a dollop of the yogurt-mango mixture on top. Garnish with cilantro, if you wish. Pass any extra yogurt-mango topping in a bowl at the table.

Quick "Barbecued" Chicken

For a couldn't-be-simpler dinner that no one can resist, try this recipe with your favorite storebought barbecue sauce or the sauce used for preparing "Barbecued" Spareribs (page 104).

Browning the chicken contributes to the taste, but the dish is still full of flavor if you don't want to take the time.   SERVES 4–6

(9–11 MINUTES UNDER HIGH PRESSURE)

2 tablespoons oil

3 to 4 pounds chicken parts, preferably thighs and drumsticks, skinned

1/2 cup water

1 1/2 cups coarsely chopped onions

1 large green bell pepper, seeded and diced (optional)

2 cups prepared barbecue sauce

Heat 1 tablespoon oil in the cooker. Brown the chicken well on both sides in small batches, adding extra oil as needed. Set the browned chicken on a platter. Pour off or sop up leftover oil, if desired.

Add the water, taking care to scrape up any browned bits sticking to the bottom.

Place the onions and green pepper (if using) in the bottom of the cooker. Add the reserved browned chicken plus any juices that have collected on the platter. Pour the sauce on top. *Do not stir.*

Lock the lid in place and over high heat bring to high pressure. Adjust the heat to maintain high pressure and cook for 9 minutes. Reduce the pressure with a quick-release method. Remove the lid, tilting it away from you to allow steam to escape.

Place the chicken on individual plates or a serving platter. If the sauce is too thin, tent the chicken with aluminum foil, and boil the sauce vigorously until reduced. Spoon the sauce on top of the chicken and serve.

Chicken Gumbo

This soupy stew, a mainstay of the Creole kitchen, is best when served in deep bowls over steamed white rice. I've eliminated the flour-oil roux that is traditionally part of the recipe; it's tricky to prepare without burning the flour, and I find that the gumbo is quite delicious without it.

The filé powder (ground sassafras leaves) stirred in at the end thickens the sauce and adds a haunting flavor that is characteristic of the dish. If you can't find filé powder, thicken the stew by slowly sprinkling a few tablespoons of fine cornmeal on top, stirring constantly while simmering gently over medium heat. SERVES 6

(9 MINUTES UNDER HIGH PRESSURE, THEN 4 MINUTES SIMMERING)

1 to 2 tablespoons olive oil

1 pound smoked sausage (such as kielbasa or French garlic), casings removed if necessary, cut into 1/2-inch slices

1 large onion, coarsely chopped

1 large green bell pepper, seeded and diced

2 celery stalks, coarsely chopped

2 large garlic cloves, minced

1/2 cup water

1 teaspoon dried thyme

2 bay leaves

1/8 teaspoon cayenne pepper, or to taste

2 1/2 to 3 pounds chicken parts, preferably drumsticks and thighs, skinned

One 28-ounce can tomatoes, coarsely chopped, including juice

10-ounce package frozen sliced baby okra

2 1/2 to 3 tablespoons filé powder

Salt and freshly ground black pepper

Heat 1 tablespoon oil in the cooker, and brown the sausage slices well on both sides in batches, adding more oil if needed. Remove half of the browned sausages and set aside.

Add the onion, green pepper, celery, and garlic, and cook over medium-high heat, stirring frequently, until the onion begins to soften, about 3 minutes. Stir in the water, thyme, bay leaves, and cayenne, taking care to scrape up any browned bits sticking to the bottom of the cooker.

Stir in the chicken. Pour the tomatoes on top. *Do not stir.*

Lock the lid in place and over high heat bring to high pressure. Adjust the heat to maintain high pressure and cook for 9 minutes. Reduce the pressure with a quick-release method. Remove the lid, tilting it away from you to allow steam to escape.

While the chicken is cooking, set the frozen okra in a strainer and pour hot water over it. When the chicken is done, stir in the okra and cook uncovered at a gentle boil until it is tender, about 4 minutes.

Turn off the heat; gradually sprinkle in the filé powder, stirring until the sauce thickens. Remove the bay leaves and add salt and pepper to taste before serving.

Brunswick Stew

This is a colorful adaptation of the tra-ditional Southern hunter's stew. No squirrel or rabbit here, but a tasty use of chicken with the requisite corn and tomatoes. For fun, I tried this recipe with sweet instead of white potatoes and thought that they added a wonderfully mellow flavor. The lima beans cooked with the chicken vir-tually dissolve to thicken the stew.

Serve the stew in soup bowls accompanied by corn bread and a fresh green salad. SERVES 4–6

(9 MINUTES UNDER HIGH PRESSURE, THEN 2–3 MINUTES SIMMERING)

1 tablespoon olive oil

1 large onion, coarsely chopped

1 cup chicken broth or water

2 bay leaves

$1/2$ teaspoon dried thyme

Generous pinch of cayenne pepper or crushed red pepper flakes

2 cups cooked or frozen baby lima beans, divided

$3^1/2$ pounds chicken parts, skinned

1 smoked ham hock

2 celery stalks, cut into 5 to 6 chunks

3 large carrots, peeled and cut into 4 to 5 chunks

$1^1/2$ pounds (about 5) medium sweet or white potatoes, peeled and halved

One 14-ounce can tomatoes, coarsely chopped, including juice

2 cups fresh or frozen (defrosted) corn kernels

$1/4$ cup finely minced fresh parsley

Salt and freshly ground black pepper

Heat the oil in the cooker. Add the onions and cook over medium-high heat until lightly browned, about 3 minutes. Add the broth, bay leaves, thyme, cayenne, half of the lima beans, the chicken parts, ham hock, celery, and carrots. Mix well, then add the potatoes. Pour the tomatoes on top. *Do not stir.*

Lock the lid in place and over high heat bring to high pressure. Adjust the heat to maintain high pressure and cook for 9 minutes. Reduce the pressure with a quick-release method. Remove the lid, tilting it away from you to allow steam to escape.

Stir in the remaining limas, corn, and parsley, and simmer until the corn and limas are tender, 2 to 3 minutes. Remove the bay leaves and ham hock. Add salt and pepper to taste.

Rock Cornish Hens Stuffed with Apricots and Prunes

Here is an easy but elegant dish to serve any time of year. For the hens to hold their shape during cooking, you'll need some kitchen string to truss them.

Depending upon your appetite and the number of accompaniments, two stuffed hens will serve either two or four people.   SERVES 2–4

(10–12 MINUTES UNDER HIGH PRESSURE)

1 to 2 tablespoons oil

2 Rock Cornish hens, about $1^{1}/_{4}$ to $1^{1}/_{2}$ pounds each

12 pitted prunes

8 dried apricots

$1/_{2}$ small lemon, cut into 6 thin slices

$1/_{4}$ cup finely minced shallots or onions

2 celery stalks, finely minced

1 cup chicken broth or bouillon

$1/_{2}$ teaspoon salt, or to taste (less if using canned broth or bouillon)

$1^{1}/_{2}$ pounds (about 4 medium) sweet potatoes, peeled and halved

1 tablespoon grated orange zest

1 to 2 teaspoons finely minced fresh ginger

$1/_{4}$ cup Grand Marnier or other orange liqueur

Heat the oil in the cooker. Brown the hens well on both sides, adding more oil if needed. Stuff each hen with 6 prunes and 4 apricots, interspersing the lemon slices among the dried fruits. Truss the hens and set aside.

In the fat remaining in the cooker, sauté the shallots and celery for 2 minutes. Stir in the broth and salt; scrape up any browned bits that are sticking to the bottom of the pan.

Place the hens side by side in the sauce. (You may need to put one hen on its side.) Place the sweet potatoes on top.

Lock the lid in place and over high heat bring to high pressure. Adjust the heat to maintain high pressure and cook for 10 minutes. Quick-release the pressure and check for doneness by inserting a knife into the drumstick joint; if the meat is still pink, nestle the lid in place, but do not lock it, and simmer until done.

Transfer the hens and all but two of the potato halves to a platter; remove the trussing. Reserve in a warm place. Add the orange zest, ginger, and Grand Marnier. Mash the potatoes left in the cooker, and boil the sauce over high heat until the alcohol burns off and the sauce is reduced and thickened slightly, 3 to 4 minutes. Adjust the seasonings. Serve in a sauceboat, or pour over the stuffed hens.

Vegetables

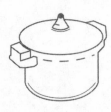

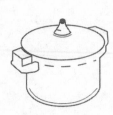

Whenever I unlock the lid and peer at a pressure-cooked soup or stew, I am always amazed at how the vegetables have maintained their color and shape—despite the fact that they may actually be meltingly soft. I also love the way they've become infused with flavor. So it should come as no surprise to you that the recipes closest to my heart in this chapter are for braised or stewed vegetables. Here is the pressure cooker performing in top form, quickly drawing the flavor out of the vegetables to create a complex sauce at the same time as it is infusing the vegetables with delicious taste.

The results are grand and the range of possibilities is enormous—from a sunny Provençal-Style Green Beans with Tomatoes to a zesty Chinese-Style Sesame Broccoli to a mellow Kale and Potatoes. And let's not forget just how good a simple dish of braised celery or leeks can be.

The pressure cooker also offers the option of quickly steaming vegetables set on a rack over water or an aromatic broth. While many cooks and old cookbooks rave about this method, I have some reservations. If you'd like to decide for yourself, see "Pressure Steaming" on page 170.

Braising—cooking vegetables in a small amount of liquid—intensifies the flavor of hard vegetables (such as Brussels sprouts, potatoes, parsnips, and turnips). Watery vegetables (such as celery, small onions, and leeks) develop irresistible taste and texture.

You'll find specific recipes for Garlic-Braised Brussels Sprouts (page 134), Braised Celery (page 146), and Braised Leeks (page 153), but if you'd like to experiment, see the Basic Recipe for Braised Vegetables on page 130.

Basic Recipe for Braised Vegetables

Use ¹/₂ cup of liquid for the vegetables that will give off a good deal of moisture as they cook, such as onions, celery, and leeks. Use 1 cup for harder vegetables like potatoes and carrots. Vegetables with the same cooking time (see Cooking Times at a Glance, page 186) may be braised together; their flavors will mingle slightly.

2 tablespoons unsalted butter or oil

1 garlic clove, finely minced (optional)

¹/₄ cup minced onions or shallots (optional)

¹/₂ to 1 cup chicken, beef, or vegetable broth (see headnote)

1 pound vegetables, trimmed and cut as directed (see alphabetical listings beginning on page 173)

1 tablespoon flour mashed into 1 tablespoon unsalted butter at room temperature (optional)

Salt and freshly ground black pepper

Heat the butter in the cooker. Sauté the garlic and onions (if using) until the onions are soft but not browned, about 3 minutes. Add the broth and vegetables.

Lock the lid in place and over high heat bring to high pressure. Set the timer, using the recipes in this chapter as a guideline for estimating cooking time. Reduce the pressure with a quick-release method. Remove the lid, tilting it away from you to allow steam to escape.

Test the vegetables for doneness. If they require more cooking, replace (but do not lock) the lid and simmer covered, over low heat, until done.

If you wish to thicken the cooking liquid and use it for sauce, remove the vegetables with a slotted spoon. Slowly whisk in small bits of the blended butter while maintaining a gentle boil. Continue cooking, stirring frequently, until the mixture thickens and the flour tastes cooked. Add salt and pepper to taste.

Green Beans with Tomatoes

I love to prepare this Provençal-style dish in the late summer, when the beans are snappy and the tomatoes full of flavor. Very fresh beans are done in a flash, but older beans can take as long as 3 minutes to become tender. If you like, stir in some torn basil leaves just before serving.　　SERVES 4–6

(30 SECONDS–3 MINUTES UNDER HIGH PRESSURE)

2 tablespoons olive oil
1 large garlic clove, minced
Generous pinch of dried or fresh rosemary leaves, chopped
1 1/2 pounds green beans, trimmed and halved crosswise
1/2 teaspoon salt, or to taste (less if using canned tomatoes)
1/3 cup water
8 to 10 ripe plum or 3 to 4 beefsteak tomatoes, peeled and coarsely
　　chopped, or substitute one 14-ounce can tomatoes, coarsely
　　chopped, including juice
Freshly ground black pepper

Heat 1 tablepoon oil in the cooker. Sauté the garlic and rosemary (if using dried) for 30 seconds, stirring constantly. Add the green beans, salt, and water. Scatter the tomatoes on top. *Do not stir.*

Lock the lid in place and over high heat bring to high pressure. Adjust the heat to maintain high pressure and cook for 30 seconds to 3 minutes as required. Reduce the pressure with a quick-release method. Remove the lid, tilting it away from you to allow steam to escape. Pass the mixture through a fine-meshed strainer, reserving the cooking liquid for broth or soup.

Add fresh rosemary (if using) and the additional tablespoon of olive oil. Adjust the seasonings before serving. Serve hot or at room temperature.

Beets à l'Orange

Citrus complements the flavor of beets and, because of the beets' striking color, this side dish is beautiful to behold.

To prepare a lightly pickled version of this dish, sauté the onion in oil rather than butter. Substitute 1/4 cup of cider vinegar for an equal amount of orange juice. Serve the pickled beets either warm or chilled.

SERVES 4

(2–3 MINUTES UNDER HIGH PRESSURE)

2 tablespoons unsalted butter or oil

1 large red onion, coarsely chopped

6 medium beets (1 1/2 to 2 pounds), halved and cut into 1/4-inch slices

1 cup orange juice

2 tablespoons maple syrup or honey (optional)

1/8 teaspoon ground allspice

Salt

Garnish: 1 teaspoon grated orange zest

Heat the butter in the cooker. Sauté the onion until limp, about 2 minutes. Add the beets, orange juice, syrup (if using), allspice, and salt to taste.

Lock the lid in place and over high heat bring to high pressure. Adjust the heat to maintain high pressure and cook for 2 minutes. Reduce the pressure with a quick-release method. Remove the lid, tilting it away from you to allow steam to escape.

If the beets require more cooking, replace the lid and steam in the residual heat for another minute or two. Adjust the seasonings. Serve in small bowls with the cooking liquid or use a slotted spoon to transfer the beets and onion to a serving platter. Garnish with orange zest.

Chinese-Style Sesame Broccoli

This quick-cooking dish proves that crisp Asian-style vegetables can emerge from a pressure cooker. No kidding. For a heartier version, brown ½ pound ground pork before adding the onion.

The timing for this recipe is based on Total Cooking Time: The count-down begins the moment the lid is locked in place. SERVES 4

(3 MINUTES TOTAL COOKING TIME)

1 head broccoli (approximately 1 to 1½ pounds)
1 tablespoon peanut or canola oil
1 large red onion, thinly sliced
1 large garlic clove, minced
1 tablespoon minced fresh ginger
2 celery stalks, cut into ½-inch slices
2 large carrots, cut into ¼-inch slices
½ cup dry sherry
½ cup vegetable broth or water
1 tablespoon soy sauce, or to taste
1 to 2 teaspoons toasted (Asian) sesame oil
Garnish: 1 to 2 tablespoons toasted sesame seeds

Cut the broccoli into florets, about 2 inches in diameter across the top. Peel and trim the stalks and cut them into ¼-inch slices. Set aside.

Heat the oil in the cooker. Add the onion and sauté for 2 minutes. Add the garlic and ginger and continue cooking, stirring occasionally, for another minute. Add the broccoli, celery, and carrots, and toss to coat with the oil. Stir in the sherry, broth, and soy sauce.

Lock the lid in place and immediately set the timer for 3 minutes. Over high heat bring toward high pressure and cook for a total of 3 minutes. Reduce any pressure with a quick-release method. Remove the lid, tilting it away from you to allow steam to escape.

If the broccoli is slightly undercooked, replace the lid and cook in the residual heat for another minute. Season to taste with sesame oil, sprinkle sesame seeds on top, and serve.

Garlic-Braised Brussels Sprouts   *Especially*
for garlic lovers. Plan on 4 minutes for small sprouts, 5 for medium. The
timing for this recipe is based on Total Cooking Time: The countdown
begins the moment the lid is locked in place and the heat is turned on.

SERVES 3–4

(4–5 MINUTES TOTAL COOKING TIME)

1 cup water
$^1/_4$ teaspoon salt
6 large garlic cloves
Generous pinch of dried thyme or dried oregano
1 pint Brussels sprouts (10 ounces), trimmed
1 tablespoon olive oil

Place the water, salt, garlic, thyme, and Brussels sprouts in the cooker.

Lock the lid in place and immediately set the timer for 4 (small or medium sprouts) or 5 minutes (large sprouts). Over high heat bring toward high pressure and cook for a total of 4 or 5 minutes. Reduce any pressure with a quick-release method. Remove the lid, tilting it away from you to allow steam to escape.

If the sprouts are not quite done, replace the lid and let them cook for a minute or two in the residual heat. When the sprouts are done, drain them (and the whole garlic cloves) and transfer to a bowl. Toss in the olive oil, adjust the seasonings, and serve.

Brussels Sprouts with Sesame Vinaigrette

grette *A sensational way to appreciate Brussels sprouts, either warm or at room temperature.*   SERVES 4

1¹/₂ pounds small Brussels sprouts, pressure-steamed until
  crisp-tender (page 176)

FOR THE SESAME VINAIGRETTE
3 tablespoons safflower or peanut oil
2 teaspoons toasted (Asian) sesame oil
2 tablespoons balsamic or other red wine vinegar
Juice of 1 lemon
¹/₂ teaspoon prepared mustard, preferably Chinese
1 teaspoon soy sauce, or to taste
Freshly ground black pepper to taste

Halve the Brussels sprouts and set them in a bowl. Combine the dressing ingredients in a jar. Shake well to blend and adjust the seasonings to taste. Pour on just enough of the dressing to thoroughly moisten the vegetables. Serve immediately or refrigerate for up to 2 days.

Cabbage with Potatoes and Leeks *This traditional Irish dish is simple to prepare in the pressure cooker. Add a nice, smoky flavor by frying 3 or 4 strips of bacon in the cooker until crisp. Set the bacon aside and use the rendered bacon fat instead of the butter or oil for sautéeing the leeks. When the dish is cooked, sprinkle the fried, crumbled bacon on top. Delicious.*

If you like this dish, try Kale and Potatoes (page 151), another winner.   SERVES 6

(5 MINUTES UNDER HIGH PRESSURE)

2 tablespoons unsalted butter or oil

1 medium leek, white part only, thoroughly rinsed and sliced (about 1 cup)

1 garlic clove, finely minced

1 cup water or vegetable broth or bouillon

2 pounds cabbage, cut into 6 to 8 wedges, core removed

1 1/2 pounds potatoes, scrubbed, halved, and cut into 1/4-inch slices

3/4 teaspoon salt, or to taste

2 to 3 tablespoons minced fresh parsley

1 to 2 tablespoons additional unsalted butter (optional)

Freshly ground black pepper

Heat the butter in the cooker. Sauté the leeks and garlic for 3 minutes. Stir in the water. Place the cabbage in the pot and top with the potatoes. Sprinkle on the salt.

Lock the lid in place and over high heat bring to high pressure. Adjust the heat to maintain high pressure and cook for 5 minutes. Reduce the pressure with a quick-release method. Remove the lid, tilting it away from you to allow steam to escape.

If the cabbage or potatoes are not quite done, replace the lid and cook in residual steam for a few more minutes. Stir in the parsley and additional butter if desired, blending the potatoes and cabbage to create a coarse, mashed potato–like mixture. Add pepper to taste and more salt, if needed.

NOTE: Since the cabbage gives up so much liquid during cooking, this recipe works in cookers that normally require more liquid to come up to pressure.

Sesame-Miso Cabbage

Miso, a salty, fermented soybean paste, adds a complex saltiness to the cabbage. The most delicious miso is unpasteurized and kept under refrigeration in health-food stores.

This dish was inspired by a recipe in The Book of Miso *by William Shurtleff and Akiko Aoyagi.* SERVES 4–6

(1 MINUTE UNDER HIGH PRESSURE)

2 tablespoons plus 1 teaspoon cider vinegar, divided

2 tablespoons miso

2 teaspoons honey

Generous pinch of ground allspice

Pinch of cayenne pepper

1/2 cup water

1 medium cabbage (about 2 1/2 pounds)

1 tablespoon vegetable oil

1 garlic clove, minced

3 large carrots, peeled and very thinly sliced on the diagonal

1 teaspoon minced fresh ginger

2 to 3 teaspoons toasted (Asian) sesame oil

2 tablespoons sesame seeds, toasted

Soy sauce or salt

In a small jar, combine 2 tablespoons vinegar, the miso, honey, allspice, cayenne, and water, and shake to blend. Quarter the cabbage, and remove and discard the core. Cut the cabbage into 1/2-inch slices.

Heat the oil in the cooker. Add the garlic and sizzle for 30 seconds, stirring constantly. Stir in the vinegar mixture, cabbage, and carrots.

Lock the lid in place and over high heat bring to high pressure. Adjust the heat to maintain high pressure and cook for 1 minute. Reduce the pressure with a quick-release method. Remove the lid, tilting it away from you to allow steam to escape.

Stir in the ginger. If the cabbage is too crunchy, replace the lid and cook for a few more minutes in the residual heat. When done, stir in sesame oil to taste plus the sesame seeds, and the additional teaspoon vinegar. Add more miso or soy sauce to taste, if desired.

NOTE: Since the cabbage gives up so much liquid during cooking, this recipe works in cookers that normally require more liquid to come up to pressure.

Sweet and Sour Red Cabbage

Four minutes is a far cry from the 1½ hours it usually takes to braise this traditional dish.

SERVES 4–6

(4 MINUTES UNDER HIGH PRESSURE)

1 medium red cabbage (about 2 pounds)
2 tablespoons unsalted butter or oil
1 large onion, coarsely chopped, preferably a red Spanish onion
2 tart apples, such as Granny Smiths, cored and cut into eighths
1/2 cup apple cider
2 tablespoons apple cider vinegar
1 tablespoon honey
1/3 cup raisins, preferably golden
1/8 teaspoon ground allspice
1/8 teaspoon salt, or to taste

Discard the tough outer leaves of the cabbage; quarter and cut away the hard core. Cut each wedge crosswise into 1/2-inch slices. Set aside.

Heat the butter in the cooker. Sauté the onions for 1 minute, stirring constantly. Add the cabbage and the remaining ingredients and stir to blend.

Lock the lid in place and over high heat bring to high pressure. Adjust the heat to maintain high pressure and cook for 4 minutes. Reduce the pressure with a quick-release method. Remove the lid, tilting it away from you to allow steam to escape.

If the cabbage is not quite tender, replace the lid and simmer over medium heat for a minute or two. Adjust the seasonings before serving.

NOTE: Since the cabbage gives up so much liquid during cooking, this recipe works in cookers that normally require more liquid to come up to pressure.

Carrot Tsimmes

This vegetarian version of the Jewish holiday dish makes a fine accompaniment to roast chicken and turkey. Sweet potatoes, carrots, prunes, and parsnips are a harmonious quartet.

SERVES 6–8

(3–4 MINUTES UNDER HIGH PRESSURE)

2 tablespoons unsalted butter

1 large onion, coarsely chopped

1 pound sweet potatoes (3 medium), peeled and cut into 6 chunks

1/2 pound parsnips, preferably slender ones, peeled and cut into 1-inch slices

5 medium carrots, peeled and cut into 1/4-inch slices

1 cup pitted prunes, coarsely chopped

Juice and zest of 1 orange

1/2 teaspoon ground cinnamon

1 cup vegetable broth or bouillon

1/4 teaspoon salt, or to taste (less if using canned broth or bouillon)

1 to 2 tablespoons lemon juice

Heat the butter in the cooker. Sauté the onions until lightly browned, about 4 minutes. Add the remaining ingredients except the lemon juice and orange zest, making sure to scrape up any browned onions sticking to the bottom of the pot.

Lock the lid in place and over high heat bring to high pressure. Adjust the heat to maintain high pressure and cook for 3 minutes. Reduce the pressure with a quick-release method. Remove the lid, tilting it away from you to allow steam to escape.

If the parsnips or carrots are not quite done, replace the lid and simmer for another minute or two. Drain off some of the cooking liquid, if desired, or mash some of the vegetables to thicken the mix. Stir in the lemon juice and orange zest, and adjust the seasonings before serving.

Curried Cauliflower and Potatoes   *I often*

order this dish in Indian restaurants. I love the fact that both the potatoes and cauliflower are soft and tender. That's just what you'll get if you cook them for 4 minutes. If you want crisper cauliflower, reduce the cooking time to 3 minutes and cut the potatoes ⅛ inch thick.   SERVES 6–8

(4 MINUTES UNDER HIGH PRESSURE)

1 medium head cauliflower (about 2¼ pounds)

3 medium potatoes (about 1¼ pounds), scrubbed

2 tablespoons peanut or canola oil

3 quarter-sized slices fresh ginger

1 teaspoon whole cumin seeds

2 teaspoons black mustard seeds (optional)

1 tablespoon plus 2 teaspoons mild curry powder

1 to 2 dried hot peppers or a pinch of cayenne pepper (optional)

½ cup water

1 teaspoon salt, or to taste

One 14-ounce can plum tomatoes, coarsely chopped, including juice

Cut the cauliflower into large florets, measuring about 2½ inches long by 2½ inches wide. Set aside. Halve the potatoes lengthwise and cut each half into ¼-inch-thick slices.

Heat the oil in the cooker. Add and sizzle the ginger, cumin seeds, and mustard seeds (if using) for 30 seconds, stirring constantly. Stir the potatoes into the oil and sauté for 1 minute, stirring constantly. Stir in the curry powder and hot pepper (if using) and cook for 10 seconds. Add the water, salt, and cauliflower. Stir to scrape up any browned bits sticking to the bottom of the cooker. Pour the tomatoes on top. *Do not stir.*

Lock the lid in place and over high heat bring to high pressure. Adjust the heat to maintain high pressure and cook for 3 or 4 minutes, according to taste. Reduce the pressure with a quick-release method. Remove the lid, tilting it away from you to allow steam to escape.

If the cauliflower or potatoes are not sufficiently cooked, replace the lid and cook in residual heat for another minute or two.

Stir well. Adjust the seasonings and serve.

Cauliflower with Hot Dill Vinaigrette

This dish is delicious hot or cold, and makes a nice substitute for a salad.

SERVES 4–6

(2–3 MINUTES UNDER HIGH PRESSURE)

3 tablespoons olive oil

3 medium leeks, white part only, thoroughly rinsed and thinly
sliced (about 2 cups)

1 garlic clove, finely minced

1 tablespoon plus 1 teaspoon white wine or sherry vinegar, divided

1 cup vegetable broth or bouillon

1 large head cauliflower, broken into large florets about 2 1/2 inches
long by 2 1/2 inches wide

1/2 cup tightly packed, finely minced fresh dill

1/4 teaspoon salt, or to taste

Heat 1 tablespoon of the oil in the cooker. Sauté the leeks and garlic for
1 minute. Stir in the 1 tablespoon of vinegar plus the broth. Add the
cauliflower and salt.

Lock the lid in place and over high heat bring to high pressure. Adjust the heat to maintain high pressure and cook for 2 minutes. Reduce
the pressure with a quick-release method. Remove the lid, tilting it
away from you to allow steam to escape.

If the cauliflower is not sufficiently cooked, replace the lid and cook
for a few more minutes in the residual heat.

Drain off about half of the cooking liquid, if desired. Toss in the dill
and the remaining olive oil, plus the teaspoon of vinegar. Adjust the
seasonings and serve either hot or at room temperature.

Mashed Celeriac and Parsnips

A superb combination using two underutilized, delicious vegetables. This is comfort food at its best, and a wonderful alternative to mashed potatoes. If parsnips are not available, use carrots cut into 1/4-inch slices.

SERVES 6

(3 MINUTES UNDER HIGH PRESSURE)

2 pounds celeriac (knob celery), peeled and cut into 1/2-inch dice
2 tablespoons lemon juice
3/4 cup vegetable or chicken broth or bouillon
1 pound slender parsnips, peeled and cut into 1-inch chunks
1 bay leaf
2 to 3 tablespoons unsalted butter
Salt

Place the diced celeriac in the cooker and pour in the lemon juice and broth. If any of the parsnip tops have diameters larger than 1 inch, cut into 2 to 3 pieces. Add the parsnips and bay leaf and stir well.

Lock the lid in place and over high heat bring to high pressure. Adjust the heat to maintain high pressure and cook for 3 minutes. Reduce the pressure with a quick-release method. Remove the lid, tilting it away from you to allow steam to escape.

If the vegetables are not quite done, replace the lid and let them cook for a minute or two in the residual heat. Remove the bay leaf and drain off most of the cooking liquid. Add butter and salt to taste, and mash with a potato masher. Transfer to a warm serving bowl and serve immediately.

NOTE: Since the celeriac gives up so much liquid during cooking, this recipe works in cookers that normally require more liquid to come up to pressure.

Braised Celery

An old-fashioned, subtle, and satisfying dish. Use only the inner tender celery stalks, as the outer ones tend to be fibrous. The timing for this recipe is based on Total Cooking Time: The countdown begins as soon as the lid is locked in place.

SERVES 4

(5 MINUTES TOTAL COOKING TIME)

2 tablespoons unsalted butter

1/4 cup minced shallots or onions

8 tender celery stalks, halved crosswise

2/3 cup chicken or vegetable broth or bouillon

1/2 teaspoon salt, or to taste (less if using canned broth or bouillon)

1 tablespoon all-purpose flour mashed into 1 tablespoon unsalted
   butter at room temperature

Heat the butter in the cooker. Sauté the shallots until soft while stirring frequently, 1 to 2 minutes. Add the celery and toss to coat with the fat. Add the broth and salt.

Lock the lid in place and immediately set the timer for 5 minutes. Over high heat bring to high pressure. Adjust the heat to maintain high pressure and cook for a total of 5 minutes. Reduce the pressure with a quick-release method. Remove the lid, tilting it away from you to allow steam to escape.

If the celery is not quite done, replace the lid and let it cook for a minute or two in the residual heat. When done, transfer the celery with a slotted spoon to a warmed platter. Thicken the sauce by gradually whisking in the blended butter while cooking at a medium boil until the sauce thickens and the flour tastes cooked, 1 to 2 minutes. Adjust the seasonings. Pour the sauce over the celery and serve.

NOTE: Since the celery gives up so much liquid during cooking, this recipe works in cookers that normally require more liquid to come up to pressure.

Collards with Bacon

This old Southern favorite is pressure-cooked to perfection in no time flat.

SERVES 4

(5–6 MINUTES UNDER HIGH PRESSURE)

1 bunch (1 to 1½ pounds) collard greens
5 strips bacon, cut into 1-inch bits
2 to 3 garlic cloves, minced
1 cup water
2 to 3 teaspoons cider vinegar
Salt, if desired

Slice off the collard stalks about 4 inches from the root end, and discard or set aside for broth. Cut the remaining part of the stalks and leaves into ¾-inch slices. Rinse thoroughly in a sinkful of water. Drain and set aside.

Fry the bacon until crisp in the cooker. Remove the crisp bacon and set aside on a paper towel to drain. Sauté the garlic in the bacon fat for 30 seconds. Add the collard greens and toss to coat with the fat. Stir in the water.

Lock the lid in place and over high heat bring to high pressure. Adjust the heat to maintain high pressure and cook for 5 minutes. Reduce the pressure with a quick-release method. Remove the lid, tilting it away from you to allow steam to escape.

Drain the collards and set in a bowl. Stir in the crisped bacon and add the cider vinegar and salt to taste, if desired.

Savory Corn Custards

These delicate individual corn custards are so elegant and festive that they belie the ease of preparation. I like to serve them right in the ½-cup ramekins used to cook them. This recipe may be doubled to serve 8; if the ramekins don't stack comfortably (pyramid fashion) in your cooker, cook in two batches. SERVES 4

(8 MINUTES UNDER HIGH PRESSURE)

Unsalted butter or oil for greasing individual ramekins
¾ cup fresh or frozen corn kernels
¾ cup milk
2 large eggs, lightly beaten
¼ cup finely minced fresh cilantro
½ teaspoon salt, or to taste

Thoroughly grease four ½-cup ramekins with butter. Divide the corn kernels equally among them. In a large measuring cup, thoroughly blend the remaining ingredients. Divide the liquid among the ramekins. Each should be about seven-eighths full.

Cover each ramekin with a large piece of aluminum foil. Leave a bit of slack at the top so that the custards can expand, and tuck the foil ends under the bottom of each ramekin. Set a rack in place and pour in 2 cups of water. Set the ramekins on the rack. To avoid cracking them, don't let any of the ramekins rest against the sides of the cooker.

Lock the lid in place and over high heat bring to high pressure. Adjust the heat to maintain high pressure and cook for 8 minutes. Reduce the pressure with a quick-release method. Remove the lid, tilting it away from you to allow steam to escape.

With a knife, make a small slit in the foil to make certain that the custard is set. If not, replace the lid and cook in residual heat for another minute or two.

With an oven mitt, carefully remove the ramekins from the cooker, then remove the foil covers. Tip off any liquid accumulated around the edges, and serve immediately.

Eggplant Ratatouille
I love to serve this hearty vegetarian stew over rice or pasta or thin it with a bit of vegetable broth or tomato juice and transform it into a soup. It is also delicious served in small bowls as a vegetable side dish.

Try stirring in a few dollops of the salty olive puree known as olivada *instead of salt: Its robustness enhances the Mediterranean flavor of the stew. Although not traditional, ratatouille is also good with some freshly grated Parmesan cheese sprinkled on top.*   SERVES 4–6

(3 MINUTES UNDER HIGH PRESSURE)

1 large eggplant (about 1¹/₂ pounds), peeled
3 tablespoons olive oil
2 garlic cloves, minced
1 cup coarsely chopped onion
1 large green bell pepper, seeded and diced
1 large red bell pepper, seeded and diced
¹/₂ cup water
1 teaspoon dried thyme or dried oregano
Pinch of sugar
1 teaspoon salt, or to taste
One 14-ounce can tomatoes, coarsely chopped, including juice
1 cup tightly packed, minced fresh basil or ¹/₄ cup minced, fresh
    flat-leaf parsley

Cut the eggplant into ¹/₂-inch-thick slices. Cut the large center slices into eighths, and cut the smaller end slices into quarters.

Heat 2 tablespoons of the oil in the cooker. Sauté the garlic, onions, and green and red peppers in the cooker until the onions are soft, about 3 minutes. Add the eggplant and toss to coat with the oil. Stir in the water, thyme, sugar, and salt. Pour the tomatoes on top. *Do not stir.*

Lock the lid in place and over high heat bring to high pressure. Adjust the heat to maintain high pressure and cook for 3 minutes. Reduce the pressure with a quick-release method. Remove the lid, tilting it away from you to allow steam to escape.

Stir in the basil and the additional tablespoon of olive oil. Adjust the seasonings. If the stew seems too thin, puree a cup or two of the mixture and stir it back into the pot, or remove the eggplant with a slotted spoon and boil the liquid vigorously until it is reduced. Serve hot or at room temperature.

Kale and Potatoes

Kale and potatoes make a superb combination, and this side dish makes wonderful comfort food for a rainy winter's day. With a quick stir at the end of cooking, the potatoes get mashed and like so many dishes prepared in the pressure cooker, this one tastes as if it's been lovingly hovered over for hours. The parsley blended in at the end gives the dish a vibrant finish.

A large head of broccoli, cut into 2-inch florets, makes a nice substitute for the kale. Reserve the stalks for another use, such as Broccoli–Corn Chowder (page 60).

To prevent a crust from forming on the bottom, set the cooker on a heat diffuser (see page 22) while cooking this dish.   SERVES 6

(5 MINUTES UNDER HIGH PRESSURE)

1 pound kale

1^{1}/$_{2}$ pounds (3 large) potatoes, scrubbed and cut into ^{1}/$_{4}$-inch slices

3 tablespoons olive oil

1 medium leek, white part only, thoroughly rinsed and thinly sliced (1 cup)

2 to 3 large garlic cloves, minced

1 large onion, coarsely chopped

4 scallions, chopped

^{3}/$_{4}$ cup water

1 teaspoon salt, or to taste

2 to 3 tablespoons finely minced fresh parsley (optional)

Cut the kale leaves from the stalks. (Reserve the stalks for the broth pot, if desired.) Rinse the leaves thoroughly, discarding any that are discolored. Cut the remaining leaves into strips about 1^{1}/$_{2}$ inches wide. Cut the potato slices in half.

Heat 2 tablespoons of the oil in the cooker. Sauté the leeks, garlic, onions, and scallions until soft, about 3 minutes. Add the water. (Watch for sputtering oil.) Beginning with a layer of kale, alternate kale and potatoes, sprinkling lightly with salt on top of each layer.

Lock the lid in place and over high heat bring to high pressure. Adjust the heat to maintain high pressure and cook for 5 minutes. Reduce the pressure with a quick-release method. Remove the lid, tilting it away from you to allow steam to escape.

Stir the mixture well so that the potatoes become slightly mashed, and add parsley (if desired). Adjust the seasonings and serve.

NOTE: Since the kale gives up so much liquid during cooking, this recipe works in cookers that normally require more liquid to come up to pressure.

Braised Leeks

If you are not acquainted with the subtle pleasures of eating leeks on their own, this simple recipe will be a taste revelation. Try it with small, tender leeks that are no larger than 1¼ inches in diameter. Allow 3 leeks per person.

The timing for this recipe is based on Total Cooking Time: The countdown begins the moment the lid is locked in place.　　　　SERVES 4

(3 MINUTES TOTAL COOKING TIME)

1 tablespoon unsalted butter
1 small garlic clove, finely minced (optional)
12 small leeks, trimmed and thoroughly rinsed (see page 180)
²/₃ cup beef, chicken, or vegetable broth or bouillon
¹/₈ teaspoon salt, or to taste
Freshly ground black pepper
1 tablespoon all-purpose flour mashed into 1 tablespoon unsalted
　　butter at room temperature

Heat the butter in the cooker. Sauté the garlic (if using) while stirring frequently for 30 seconds. Add the leeks and toss to coat with the butter. Add the broth, salt, and pepper to taste.

Lock the lid in place and immediately set the timer for 3 minutes. Over high heat bring toward high pressure and cook for a total of 3 minutes. Reduce any pressure with a quick-release method. Remove the lid, tilting it away from you to allow steam to escape.

Remove to a warmed platter. Thicken the sauce by gradually whisking in the blended butter while cooking at a medium boil until the sauce thickens and the flour tastes cooked, 1 to 2 minutes. Adjust the seasonings, pour the sauce over the leeks, and serve.

Okra and Tomato Stew

If there's ever a dull moment in the conversation, mention the word okra and you're sure to get a quick response. People either love or hate this vegetable, and most of it comes down to whether or not they enjoy its unusual texture.

Make another version of this dish by rendering the fat from 4 to 5 slices (about 2 ounces) of diced bacon at the beginning of cooking, then using the bacon fat instead of olive oil. Garnish with the crisped bacon after the stew is cooked.

Serve over white or brown rice.   SERVES 4

(2–3 MINUTES UNDER HIGH PRESSURE)

2 tablespoons olive oil

Large pinch of crushed red pepper flakes

2 large garlic cloves

1 cup coarsely chopped onions

1 bay leaf

1/2 cup water

1 tablespoon cider vinegar

1/4 teaspoon salt, or to taste

10 ounces fresh or frozen (defrosted) okra, preferably about
    2 inches long

1 pound fresh plum or beefsteak tomatoes, peeled and coarsely
    chopped, or one 28-ounce can tomatoes, coarsely chopped,
    including juice

3/4 cup tightly packed minced fresh basil or 1/3 cup minced parsley
    or cilantro

Freshly ground black pepper

Heat the oil in the cooker. Add the red pepper flakes, garlic, and onion, and sauté for 3 minutes. Stir in the bay leaf, water, vinegar, and salt, taking care to scrape up any browned bits stuck to the bottom of the cooker.

Add the okra. Pour the tomatoes on top. *Do not stir.*

Lock the lid in place and over high heat bring to high pressure. Adjust the heat to maintain high pressure and cook for 2 minutes. Reduce the pressure with a quick-release method. Remove the lid, tilting it away from you to allow steam to escape. If the okra is not quite done, replace the lid and cook for a minute or two in the residual heat.

Stir in the basil and pepper to taste. Adjust the seasonings and serve.

Potatoes Paprika   *A fast version of a savory classic.*

SERVES 6

(3 MINUTES UNDER HIGH PRESSURE)

1 tablespoon unsalted butter or oil

1 large garlic clove, minced

1/2 pound mushrooms, sliced

2 pounds (4 to 5 large) russet or Yukon gold potatoes, scrubbed,
    halved, and cut into 1/4-inch slices

1/2 pound (6 to 7) small white onions, peeled and halved
    (frozen are fine)

1 cup chicken or vegetable broth or bouillon

1/2 teaspoon dried rosemary leaves

1 bay leaf

1 tablespoon tomato paste

2 to 3 teaspoons paprika, preferably Spanish or Hungarian

3/4 teaspoon salt, or to taste (less if using canned broth or bouillon)

Freshly ground black pepper

1 cup sour cream or plain yogurt

Heat the butter in the cooker. Sauté the garlic and mushrooms for 1 minute, stirring frequently. Stir in the potatoes and onions. Combine the broth, rosemary, bay leaf, tomato paste, paprika, salt, and pepper to taste. Pour into the cooker and stir.

Lock the lid in place and over high heat bring to high pressure. Adjust the heat to maintain high pressure and cook for 3 minutes. Reduce the pressure with a quick-release method. Remove the lid, tilting it away from you to allow steam to escape.

Remove the bay leaf and ladle out about 1/2 cup of hot liquid from the cooker. Stir the sour cream into the hot liquid, then stir this mixture back into the pot. Adjust the seasonings before serving.

New (Red) Potatoes with Rosemary, Garlic, and Olives

A very quick and delicious way to prepare small, waxy, red potatoes. If you use larger red potatoes, cut them in half or lengthen the pressure-cooking time.

SERVES 4

(4–5 MINUTES UNDER HIGH PRESSURE)

2 tablespoons olive oil

2 large garlic cloves, minced

Generous pinch of dried rosemary leaves

1 pound *very* small red potatoes (about 16 with a 1½-inch diameter), scrubbed

¼ cup oil-cured black olives, pitted and coarsely chopped

1 cup vegetable broth or bouillon

Salt

Garnishes: minced fresh parsley and freshly grated Parmesan (optional)

Heat 1 tablespoon of the olive oil in the cooker. Sauté the garlic and rosemary for 10 seconds, then add the potatoes and toss to coat with the oil. Add the olives and broth.

Lock the lid in place and over high heat bring to high pressure. Adjust the heat to maintain high pressure and cook for 4 minutes. Reduce the pressure with a quick-release method. Remove the lid, tilting it away from you to allow steam to escape.

If the potatoes aren't quite done, replace the lid and simmer over low heat for another minute or two.

Pass the mixture through a fine-mesh strainer and discard the cooking liquid (or save it for your next soup). Set the potatoes in a bowl. Add the remaining tablespoon of olive oil, and adjust the seasonings, adding salt to taste. Garnish with parsley and Parmesan, or serve grated cheese on the side, if you wish.

Bourbon-Laced Sweet Potatoes *Cooking*

sweet potatoes with orange juice and marmalade quickly creates a sweet and festive holiday dish. SERVES 4–6

(2 MINUTES UNDER HIGH PRESSURE)

3/4 cup orange juice

1/4 cup bourbon (or substitute additional orange juice)

1/2 teaspoon ground cinnamon

5 large sweet potatoes (3 pounds), peeled and cut into 1/4-inch slices

1/3 cup orange marmalade

2 to 3 tablespoons unsalted butter, cut into bits

1/8 teaspoon grated nutmeg

Salt

1/3 cup coarsely chopped walnuts

Combine the orange juice, bourbon, and cinnamon in the cooker. Place the sweet potato slices in the liquid and top with the marmalade. *Do not stir.*

Lock the lid in place and over high heat bring to high pressure. Adjust the heat to maintain high pressure and cook for 2 minutes. Reduce the pressure with a quick-release method. Remove the lid, tilting it away from you to allow steam to escape.

Adjust the seasonings, adding the butter, nutmeg, and salt to taste as you stir in the walnuts and create a coarse mash. Transfer to a heated serving bowl and serve immediately or reheat in a medium 350-degree Fahrenheit oven when needed.

Mashed Rutabagas and Potatoes

This simple and homey preparation goes perfectly with a traditional roast. The potato tones down the assertive flavor of the rutabaga.

Use a fork to mash the vegetables—the mixture tends to get gummy in the food processor. I love it coarse and lumpy, but that's a matter of personal taste.

SERVES 4–6

(6–8 MINUTES UNDER HIGH PRESSURE)

2 to 4 tablespoons unsalted butter
1 medium onion, coarsely chopped
1 cup vegetable broth or bouillon
1 small rutabaga (1 1/2 pounds), peeled, quartered, and cut into
   1/2-inch slices
1 1/2 pounds (3 large) potatoes, peeled and quartered
3/4 teaspoon salt, or to taste (less if using canned broth or bouillon)
Freshly ground black pepper (optional)

Heat 2 tablespoons of the butter in the cooker. Sauté the onion until lightly browned, stirring frequently, about 4 minutes. Pour the vegetable broth into the cooker. Add the rutabaga, potatoes, salt, and pepper.

Lock the lid in place and over high heat bring to high pressure. Adjust the heat to maintain high pressure and cook for 6 minutes. Reduce the pressure with a quick-release method. Remove the lid, tilting it away from you to allow steam to escape.

Transfer the mixture to a bowl, and mash with a fork, mixing in the remaining butter, salt, and pepper to taste.

Simple Squash Puree

This is not so much a recipe as a reminder, since it is so easy to overlook the simplest things in our quest for the exotic. While testing recipes for this book, I had some leftover cooked acorn and butternut squash and made a great rediscovery. Pureed, cooked squash with a tiny bit of butter blended in is just heavenly, and its color is the brightest orange of an autumn leaf.

I like to serve pureed squash plain, but you can add some salt, pepper, cinnamon, ginger, or freshly grated nutmeg. One warning: Cold squash is just awful, so if it isn't just-cooked, heat before serving.

For details on pressure-steaming various types of squash, see page 184.

Gingered Butternut Squash with Pineapple

This lovely fall dish is an excellent accompaniment to roast turkey, ham, or pork. The oats thicken the sauce and give it a smooth texture. Peeling the squash is optional since the pressure does a fine job of softening the skin.

SERVES 4–6

(3 MINUTES UNDER HIGH PRESSURE)

1 medium butternut squash (about 1 1/2 pounds), halved, seeded, and cut into 1/2-inch slices

2 to 3 tablespoons unsalted butter or oil

1 large Spanish (red) onion, coarsely chopped

3/4 teaspoon ground ginger

One 3-inch cinnamon stick, broken in two

1/4 cup old-fashioned rolled oats

Generous pinch of salt

One 20-ounce can pineapple chunks in unsweetened pineapple juice, drained, juice reserved

Water

Cut the squash slices in half and then in half again to create chunks about 1/2 inch thick and 1 1/2 inches long. Set aside.

Heat the butter in the cooker. Sauté the onion for 1 minute, then stir in the ginger, cinnamon sticks, oats, and salt. Add enough water to the reserved pineapple juice to equal 2/3 cup, then pour on top. *Do not stir.* Add the squash.

Lock the lid in place and over high heat bring to high pressure. Adjust the heat to maintain high pressure and cook for 3 minutes. Reduce the pressure with a quick-release method. Remove the lid, tilting it away from you to allow steam to escape.

Remove the cinnamon sticks. Stir in the pineapple chunks, replace the lid, and simmer until the pineapple is hot and the squash is cooked to desired consistency, an additional 30 to 60 seconds. Adjust the seasonings and serve.

Autumn Stew

A simple medley of fall-winter vegetables for those who enjoy clean and pure flavors. You can vary the amounts and proportions of the vegetables as you like; just cut them all into slices approximately ½ inch thick. Serve the mixed vegetables as a side dish. Transform any leftovers into a delicious soup by pureeing with vegetable broth. SERVES 6

(3-4 MINUTES UNDER HIGH PRESSURE)

1 cup vegetable broth or water

3 to 4 parsnips, peeled and sliced

2 to 3 carrots, peeled and sliced

2 medium sweet potatoes, peeled and sliced

1½ pounds butternut or Hubbard squash, peeled, halved, seeded, and cut into ½-inch slices

½ teaspoon salt, or to taste

1 to 2 tablespoons unsalted butter

Grated nutmeg

Pour the broth into the cooker and add the vegetables. Sprinkle on the salt.

Lock the lid in place and over high heat bring to high pressure. Adjust the heat to maintain high pressure and cook for 3 minutes. Reduce the pressure with a quick-release method. Remove the lid, tilting it away from you to allow steam to escape.

If the vegetables are not tender, replace the lid (but don't lock it) and simmer until done. Lift the vegetables out of the cooker with a slotted spoon. Stir the butter into the vegetables and season to taste with salt and grated nutmeg.

Granola-Stuffed Acorn Squash

Choose a flavorful granola with raisins and nuts to use as a ready-made stuffing for acorn squash. For color, garnish each mound of granola with a few carrot slices.

Since acorn squash is rather bland, enhance the taste with a liberal sprinkling of cinnamon and salt before filling.

MAKES 2 LARGE OR 4 SMALL PORTIONS

(6 MINUTES UNDER HIGH PRESSURE)

1 cup granola
$1/4$ to $1/2$ teaspoon ground ginger
$1/2$ cup apple juice or water
1 acorn squash (about $1^3/4$ pounds), halved horizontally
1 to 2 tablespoons honey
Cinnamon
Salt
1 tablespoon unsalted butter, cut in two
Garnish: 4 to 6 carrot slices (optional)

In a small bowl, stir together the granola and $1/4$ teaspoon of the ginger. Stir in the juice and set aside to soften slightly.

Meanwhile, prepare the squash halves by scraping out the seeds. Cut the stem and bottom ends so that each half will sit flat. Brush or drizzle honey on the fleshy surface of the squash halves and dust liberally with cinnamon and salt to taste. Set a small piece of butter into each cavity.

Taste the granola mixture and if needed, add more ginger. Place half the mixture into each cavity, and arrange the carrot slices (if using) decoratively on top. Place the steaming rack in the cooker and pour in 1 to 2 cups of water (depending upon the manufacturer's recommended minimum). Set the stuffed squash halves on the rack. You may need to wedge one so that it rests on the edge of the other, leaning against one side of the cooker.

Lock the lid in place and over high heat bring to high pressure. Adjust the heat to maintain high pressure and cook for 6 minutes. Reduce the pressure with a quick-release method. Remove the lid, tilting it away from you to allow steam to escape.

Lift the squash from the cooker and serve as is, or carefully divide each half in two, pressing the filling into place with the back of a fork or spoon.

Seven-Minute Summer Tomato Sauce

I like to make this sauce when tomatoes are bursting with flavor and falling off the vine. There is so much liquid in the tomatoes that there is no need to add water.

Sometimes I omit the salt and add a tablespoon of the Italian olive paste, olivada, *after the sauce is cooked: heavenly.*

MAKES APPROXIMATELY 4 CUPS

(7 MINUTES UNDER HIGH PRESSURE)

2 tablespoons fruity olive oil

1 cup coarsely chopped onions

1 large garlic clove, minced

3 pounds ripe plum or beefsteak tomatoes, peeled if desired, cored, and cut into chunks

1/2 teaspoon salt, or to taste

1/2 cup tightly packed fresh basil

Heat the oil in the cooker. Sauté the onions and garlic for 3 minutes, stirring frequently. Add the tomatoes and salt. *Do not stir.*

Lock the lid in place and over high heat bring to high pressure. Adjust the heat to maintain high pressure and cook for 7 minutes. Reduce the pressure by placing the cooker under cold running water. Remove the lid, tilting it away from you to allow steam to escape. If the sauce is too thin, either strain out about 1 cup of the liquid (it can be used in soups or vegetable broths) or boil, uncovered, until reduced to desired consistency. If you have used unpeeled tomatoes, pass the sauce through a food mill or pulse in a food processor, if you wish.

Stir in the basil and additional salt, if needed.

Tomato Sauce with Hot Pork Sausage

Here's a 20-minute sauce with 2-hour flavor. You can substitute ground beef or veal for the sausage or eliminate the meat entirely for a vegetarian version—just season with a heavier hand and add some crushed red pepper flakes, if you want to give the sauce some heat.

When I make tomato sauce, I always like to prepare extra for the freezer, so this recipe makes enough to feed a small army. You can easily cut the quantities in half.   MAKES 3½ QUARTS

(20 MINUTES UNDER HIGH PRESSURE)

1 to 2 tablespoons olive oil

3 large garlic cloves, minced

2 cups coarsely chopped onions

1 pound fresh hot Italian pork sausage, casings removed if
   necessary

1/2 cup water

2 celery stalks, finely chopped

1 large carrot, finely chopped

2 teaspoons dried oregano

1 teaspoon dried rosemary leaves

1 teaspoon fennel seeds

2 bay leaves

1 teaspoon salt, or to taste

Three 28-ounce cans tomatoes, coarsely chopped, including juice

Two 6-ounce cans tomato paste

Freshly ground black pepper

Heat 1 tablespoon oil in the cooker. Sauté the garlic and onions for 3 minutes, adding an extra tablespoon of oil if needed. Stir in the sausage, breaking it up into small pieces with a spoon. Brown the sausage thoroughly. Stir in the water, taking care to scrape up any browned bits sticking to the bottom of the cooker. Add the celery, carrot, oregano, rosemary, fennel seeds, bay leaves, and salt.

Pour the tomatoes on top and plop tablespoons of the tomato paste over them. *Do not stir.*

Lock the lid in place and over high heat bring to high pressure. Adjust the heat to maintain high pressure and cook for 20 minutes. Let the pressure drop naturally or quick-release by placing the cooker under cold running water. Remove the lid, tilting it away from you to allow steam to escape.

Remove the bay leaves. Stir well, and adjust the seasonings, adding black pepper to taste. If the sauce is too thin, boil it uncovered until reduced to the desired consistency. Serve immediately or cool to room temperature and refrigerate or freeze until needed.

Turnips with Orange-Mustard Sauce

Orange juice and mustard in conjunction with prunes and ginger give this dish a sweet, pickled taste. It gets rave reviews, served either hot or at room temperature.   SERVES 4–6

(2 MINUTES UNDER HIGH PRESSURE)

2 tablespoons unsalted butter or oil, divided

2 teaspoons finely minced fresh ginger

1½ pounds medium turnips (about 6), peeled and quartered

⅓ cup coarsely chopped, pitted prunes

1 cup orange juice

1 tablespoon Dijon-style mustard

Salt

Heat 1 tablespoon of the butter in the cooker. Add and sizzle the ginger for 10 seconds, stirring constantly. Stir in the turnips and prunes, and toss to coat with the butter. Combine the orange juice and mustard, and pour over the turnips.

Lock the lid in place and over high heat bring to high pressure. Adjust the heat to maintain high pressure and cook for 2 minutes. Reduce the pressure with a quick-release method. Remove the lid, tilting it away from you to allow steam to escape.

Drain off some of the cooking liquid, if desired. Stir in the extra tablespoon of butter and salt to taste before serving.

Turnips and Apples
A lovely dish to serve at any fall or winter holiday celebration. The grated apples cook into a delicate sweet sauce, thickened slightly by the oats.

SERVES 4

(1–2 MINUTES UNDER HIGH PRESSURE)

2 tablespoons unsalted butter

2 celery stalks, thinly sliced

1 pound apples, cored, peeled, and grated (about 2¼ cups)

³⁄₄ cup apple juice or cider

2 tablespoons old-fashioned rolled oats

¹⁄₂ teaspoon ground cinnamon

Generous pinch of freshly grated nutmeg

Pinch of salt

¹⁄₃ cup raisins or currants

1¼ pounds (4 large) turnips, peeled, halved, and cut into ¼-inch slices

1 to 2 tablespoons fresh lemon juice

Heat the butter in the cooker. Toss in the celery and sauté for 1 minute, stirring frequently. Add the apples, apple juice, oats, cinnamon, nutmeg, salt, raisins, and turnips, and stir to blend.

Lock the lid in place and over high heat bring to high pressure. Adjust the heat to maintain high pressure; cook for 1 minute for crunchy turnips and 2 minutes for soft turnips. Reduce the pressure with a quick-release method. Remove the lid, tilting it away from you to allow steam to escape.

Adjust the seasonings, adding fresh lemon juice to bring up the flavors.

NOTE: Since the apples give off so much liquid during cooking, this recipe works in cookers that normally require more liquid to come up to pressure.

PRESSURE STEAMING

The conventional way to pressure-cook plain fresh vegetables is to set them on a rack above the water and steam them. Certain vegetables—sliced carrots or baby okra, for example—take so well to steam heat that they emerge from the cooker with enhanced flavor. For variety, try steaming vegetables over an aromatic broth (see page 171), which not only contributes subtle flavor, but fills the kitchen with an irresistible fragrance.

For preparing a large quantity of longer-cooking vegetables like beets or whole pattypan squash, the efficiency of the pressure cooker can't be beat. Pressure-steaming is also a great way to set time records for cooking quartered potatoes, winter squash, and turnips that are to be mashed or pureed.

I don't recommend the pressure cooker for all steaming tasks. I seriously question the value of pressure-steaming quick-cooking vegetables such as asparagus or fresh young corn when the savings in time is negligible and the danger of overcooking is enormous.

For those of you who like to pressure-steam, I've compiled some general guidelines to help you along. Detailed information on pressure-steaming each vegetable is included in the alphabetical listing that begins on page 173 and in Cooking Times at a Glance on page 186.

If your cooker doesn't come with a steaming basket, you can use an inexpensive collapsible steaming basket as a substitute.

Basic Guidelines for Steaming Vegetables

1. Trim and prepare the vegetable as directed in the individual alphabetical entries. Vegetables with the same cooking times may be steamed together.

2. Pour in the minimum amount of liquid required by your cooker's manufacturer and turn the heat to high.

3. Set the steaming basket in place.

4. Unless otherwise stated in the alphabetical listing below, distribute the vegetables evenly in the steaming basket.

5. Lock the lid in place, set the timer, and cook according to times indicated in Cooking Times at a Glance (see page 186).

6. *Always use the quick-release method after cooking vegetables, which can be quite delicate and easily overcooked.*

Aromatic Steaming Broths

When steaming fresh vegetables in the pressure cooker, with little extra effort you can enhance taste by using an aromatic broth: The herbs and seasonings in the steaming water gently infuse the vegetables with flavor as they are cooking. Think of the steaming water as a mini-broth, and add whatever flavorful ingredients are at hand.

Use the savory broth when steaming green vegetables, including Brussels sprouts, artichokes, green beans, and okra. The spice-scented broth is more suited to squash, sweet potatoes, turnips, carrots, and parsnips. Use the minimum amount of water required by your cooker's manufacturer. Feel free to omit any of the ingredients except, of course, the water.

Savory Steaming Broth

1 cup water

1 garlic clove, coarsely chopped

1 small onion or a few scallions or leek greens, coarsely chopped

Small bunch of parsley sprigs or stems

1 bay leaf

Combine the ingredients in the cooker. Set the steaming rack or basket in place and add the vegetables. Proceed according to directions for individual vegetables.

Spice-Scented Broth

1 cup water

1 cinnamon stick, broken in two

5 whole cloves

4 crushed cardamom pods

1/4 teaspoon whole, crushed allspice or 1/8 teaspoon ground allspice

Combine the ingredients in the cooker. Set the steaming rack or basket in place and add the vegetables. Proceed according to directions for individual vegetables.

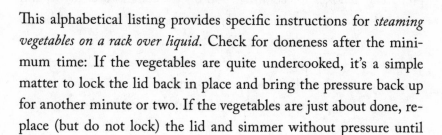 VEGETABLES A TO Z

This alphabetical listing provides specific instructions for *steaming vegetables on a rack over liquid*. Check for doneness after the minimum time: If the vegetables are quite undercooked, it's a simple matter to lock the lid back in place and bring the pressure back up for another minute or two. If the vegetables are just about done, replace (but do not lock) the lid and simmer without pressure until done.

TOTAL COOKING TIME

The extra minute it might take for the cooker to reach high pressure could easily overcook delicate vegetables, so for these vegetables I calculate Total Cooking Time instead of time under high pressure. In this system, the vegetables are set on a rack over *boiling* water, and the *countdown begins the moment the lid is locked in place*.

Remember: *Timing is always based on setting vegetables over water that is already boiling.*

ARTICHOKES

- Large (9–10 ounces): 9–11 minutes under high pressure
- Medium (6–8 ounces): 6–8 minutes under high pressure
- Baby (1 ounce each): 3–4 minutes under high pressure

Pressure-steamed artichokes are terrific! Use at least 1 cup water (or manufacturer's recommended liquid minimum) to steam artichokes. Savory Steaming Broth (page 172) is highly recommended and after cooking can be strained, reduced through vigorous boiling, and used for a dipping sauce with the addition of butter or olive oil, fresh lemon juice, and salt to taste.

For best results use medium artichokes; the outer leaves of large ones can become overcooked by the time the heart is tender. To prepare artichokes for cooking, pull off the tough outer leaves and slice about an inch off the top. Trim the bottoms so the artichokes sit flat on the steaming rack. Depending upon the shape of your cooker, 3 to 4 artichokes will fit comfortably, side by side. They can also be "pyramided," but avoid having any touch the sides of the pot, and don't fill the pot higher than is recommended by the manufacturer.

Artichokes are properly cooked when an inner leaf pulls off with a gentle tug and its flesh can be easily scraped off. If the artichokes are quite undercooked after initial cooking time is up, lock the lid back in place and return to high pressure for another 1 to 2 minutes. If the artichokes are almost done, replace the lid and simmer without pressure for another minute or two.

ASPARAGUS

- Average asparagus: 1½–2 minutes total cooking time
- Pencil asparagus: 60–90 seconds total cooking time

Trim the asparagus by snapping off the woody ends. Peel the stalks below the tips, if desired. Rinse quickly.

Spread out the spears as much as possible. When cooking a large quantity, pile them on top of each other.

If slightly underdone, lock the lid back in place and steam in the residual heat for an additional minute or two.

BEANS, GREEN (STRING)

- Whole: 2–3 minutes total cooking time
- Halved: 2–3 minutes total cooking time

Trim the beans by slicing off the tops and tails. Cut in half or thirds crosswise. Rinse thoroughly.

Spread out the beans as much as possible. When cooking a large quantity, pile them on top of each other.

If slightly underdone, replace the lid and steam in residual heat for an additional minute or two. Older beans may require cooking under high pressure for 1 to 3 minutes.

BEETS

- Medium–large whole (5–6 ounces each): 20–22 minutes under high pressure
- Small, whole (3–4 ounces each): 11–13 minutes under high pressure
- ¼-inch slices: 3–5 minutes under high pressure
- Young beet greens: 2–3 minutes total cooking time

Cut off the beet greens, leaving 1 inch of the stem attached. Scrub the beets well. Except perhaps for aesthetic reasons, you don't have to peel beets since the pressure cooker tenderizes their skins. If you peel them, it's much easier to do so after they're cooked; just trim off the tops and slip off the skins with your fingers—or use a paper towel to avoid staining your hands.

Spread out the beets evenly on the rack. If cooking in quantity, pyramid the layers, but be mindful of your cooker's maximum fill line. Properly cooked beets are fork-tender right through to their centers.

Coarsely chopped beet greens cook quickly and make flavorful, last-minute additions to soups and stews. Young beet greens are delicious when prepared like spinach.

BROCCOLI

- Large florets (3½ inches across the top): 2–3 minutes total cooking time
- Stalks, peeled, cut into ¼-inch slices: 3–4 minutes total cooking time

- Stalks, peeled, cut into ⅛-inch slices: 2–3 minutes total cooking time

Florets and stalks cook at different rates. To cook them together, use large florets and cut the stalks into very thin slices.

Peel the stalks, if desired, or rinse thoroughly.

BROCCOLI PUREE

To prepare a tasty broccoli puree, sizzle a minced clove of garlic in 3 to 4 tablespoons of olive oil until lightly browned, about 30 seconds. Puree a cooked bunch of broccoli, adding the garlic, olive oil, and a bit of water or chicken or vegetable broth to thin it slightly. You can also blend in up to a cupful of leftover cooked potatoes or rice. Season with salt, freshly ground pepper, and nutmeg to taste. Reheat thoroughly before serving.

BRUSSELS SPROUTS

- Large (about 2 inches long): 4–5 minutes total cooking time
- Small (about 1½ inches long): 3–4 minutes total cooking time

Trim the bottoms and remove any yellowed, torn, or brown-edged outside leaves. With the tip of a small knife, cut a shallow "x" into each bottom. Rinse thoroughly.

For best results, select only small, very fresh sprouts. Unfortunately, Brussels sprouts are usually sold in 10-ounce pints and sizes often vary considerably within each pint. To accommodate this variation, either separate large and small sprouts and cook them separately or cook the sprouts together for 3 minutes, then remove the small ones and cook the large ones an additional minute. (Halving large sprouts usually results in slight overcooking.)

Older sprouts take considerably longer to cook than young, fresh ones. Since overcooked sprouts are ghastly, you're better off erring on the side of undercooking them. You can always set the lid back in place for a few extra minutes of steaming in the residual heat.

CABBAGE, WHITE OR SAVOY

- 1 large cabbage (about 3 pounds), quartered: 3–4 minutes total cooking time
- Coarsely shredded: 90 seconds total cooking time

Remove the outer leaves and quarter the cabbage. Slice the core from each quarter and discard.

Cooked cabbage should be pale yellow-green and slightly crunchy. Overcooked cabbage develops a strong and unpleasant taste and odor. When in doubt, quick-release the pressure early and finish off by simmering.

RED CABBAGE

I don't recommend pressure-cooking red cabbage on its own, since it requires contact with an acid substance to retain its color. Try Sweet and Sour Red Cabbage (page 140).

CARROTS

- Large carrots, whole, 6–8 minutes under high pressure
- Large carrots, cut into 2-inch chunks: 4–5 minutes under high pressure
- ¼-inch slices: 1 minute under high pressure

Trim carrot tops and root ends. If the carrots are well scrubbed and thinly sliced, peeling them is unnecessary, but peel them for aesthetic reasons if you like. For maximum flavor, steam carrots whole, then slice them after cooking. They retain their shape and color beautifully in the pressure cooker, even if slightly overcooked.

CAULIFLOWER

- Large florets (about 2½ inches across the top): 2–3 minutes total cooking time

Cut away the outer leaves of the cauliflower and break the florets off the central stalk, aiming for florets of roughly equal size. Cut very large florets into 2 pieces. Peel the floret stems, if desired. Rinse well.

CELERIAC (CELERY ROOT, KNOB CELERY)

- ½-inch dice: 3–4 minutes total cooking time

A primordial-looking, brown-skinned knob with many roots extending from one end, celery root tastes perfectly civilized: a bit like the heart of celery but more starchy. It's a delicious vegetable and deserves better recognition, particularly since it contains more fiber, iron, and B vitamins than celery.

Buy the smallest specimens you can find, as the larger ones tend to be spongy in the center. First cut off the two ends, then attack the peel with a sharp peeler. Slice as the recipe directs. Peeled celeriac has a tendency to brown upon exposure to air, so set the pieces in water or broth doused with a few tablespoons of lemon juice.

Try dicing or pureeing plain, steamed celeriac. Toss in butter, and season with salt and freshly ground white pepper to taste. Highly recommended.

CELERY

- 1-inch slices: 3–4 minutes total cooking time

Trim celery; remove tough strings if using large stalks. Aside from preparing braised celery, I can't think of any reason to cook it alone, but sliced or chopped celery adds valuable flavor to soups, stews, and rice pilafs prepared in the pressure cooker.

CHESTNUTS

- Fresh, with shell intact: 5–6 minutes under high pressure
- Peeled and dried: 15 minutes under high pressure

With the tip of a paring knife, score a shallow "x" on the flat side of the shell of each fresh chestnut.

Do not use the rack for cooking chestnuts. Bring 2 quarts of water to a boil in the cooker, then add the chestnuts.

To test doneness, remove a chestnut with a slotted spoon. Peel off its shell and brown paperlike inner skin. A well-cooked chestnut is soft and has little to no crunch. Chestnuts can be a real nuisance to peel, especially if they've been refrigerated, so peel them while they're still warm.

Shelled dried chestnuts cook quickly in the pressure cooker. They have a slight smokiness and are delicious; look for them in gourmet shops and health-food stores. For each cup of dried chestnuts, use 3 cups of water. After cooking, save the liquid for making a soup or stew.

Chestnuts are traditionally used in stuffings, but are also wonderful to cook with grains or wild rice. If this idea appeals to you, see Brown Rice with Chestnuts, Prunes, and Apricots (page 224).

COLLARDS (SEE GREENS)

CORN

- Corn on the cob (old, large): 3½–4 minutes total cooking time
- Corn on the cob (young, fresh): 2–3 minutes total cooking time

Remove the husks and silks. Use your manufacturer's recommended minimum amount of water under the rack, and set 4 to 5 husks on the rack. The husks impart a delicate, sweet flavor to the corn.

Break the cobs in half, if necessary, to fit in the cooker. Layer in pyramid fashion on top of the husks.

EGGPLANT

- Eggplant, cut into 1½-inch chunks: 2–3 minutes total cooking time

Steam eggplant only when you want to make a quick puree. It's best to peel it; the skin doesn't soften sufficiently during the brief cooking time.

GREENS (BEET, COLLARDS, KALE)

- Beet greens: 2–3 minutes total cooking time
- Collards: 5–6 minutes under high pressure
- Kale: 1–2 minutes under high pressure

Wash greens very well in a sinkful of water. Discard tough, old, or yellowed leaves. Cut away stems and ribs of larger leaves. Roll up large leaves and slice them crosswise. Thinly slice stems into 1-inch lengths. Discard stems that are thick and fibrous.

Since steaming sometimes brings out a sour taste, I much prefer to braise greens in oil or bacon fat with a little broth and finish them off with a sprinkling of lemon juice or vinegar.

KALE (SEE GREENS)

LEEKS

- Large whole leeks (over 1½-inch diameter): 3–4 minutes total cooking time
- Small whole leeks (under 1¼-inch diameter): 2–3 minutes total cooking time

Cut off the greens parts (which can be reserved for broth), and cut about halfway down the center of the white part in the direction of the root. Under cold running water, gently separate the layers to wash away any sand. Trim off and discard the root end. Drain thoroughly.

Perfectly cooked leeks are fork-tender, but retain just a bit of crunch. If you are adding leeks to a soup, you can use the whole leek, including the dark green parts; the "pc" does a great job of tenderizing them and the dark parts of the leaves are full of flavor.

MUSTARD GREENS (SEE GREENS)

OKRA

- Whole small, tender pods: 2–3 minutes total cooking time

I'm convinced that most people who don't like okra have never tasted it properly cooked. Keep its gooeyness under control by selecting only the small pods. They are tender and can be cooked whole; just be sure to trim them on the line where the stem meets the pod.

Properly cooked okra is slightly crunchy and bright green.

ONIONS

- Medium-small white (2 ounces each): 4–5 minutes under high pressure
- Small white (½ ounce each): 2–3 minutes under high pressure

Unless otherwise stated, recipes calling for small white refer to those onions that are double or triple the size of tiny pearl onions. Look for firm, white onions with tight-fitting skins. Trim the onions and strip off the skins.

When recipes call for chopped onions, use the common yellow onion.

PARSNIPS

- 1-inch chunks: 2–4 minutes under high pressure
- ¼-inch slices: 10–60 seconds under high pressure

Look for young, slender parsnips; old, thick ones tend to be woody. Trim the tops and root ends, and peel. When cutting larger parsnips into chunks or slices, cut the wider-topped slices into 2 or 3 pieces.

Parsnips don't cook evenly when steamed over water; the outside tends to be overcooked by the time the inside is done. This is particularly true of chunks larger than 1 inch. But they do cook to mellow perfection and keep their shape beautifully when braised or cooked in soups and stews.

I'm crazy about parsnips, and am very partial to their subtle sweetness. A special favorite recipe is Curried Parsnip Soup (page 50).

POTATOES, WHITE

- Large, whole Yukon golds: 25–30 minutes under high pressure
- Medium, quartered: 5–7 minutes under high pressure
- ¼-inch slices: 2–3 minutes under high pressure

I often leave the thin skins on russet (baking) and boiling potatoes, as I like their flavor, but they must be well scrubbed. The "pc" tenderizes the skin, and you'll be amazed at how, when cooked in soups and stews, the potatoes become infused with flavor, even when their jackets are on.

Consider surrounding a pot roast or brisket with whole potatoes and cooking the potatoes for the entire hour or so. (Before cooking, pierce them in a few places to prevent the skins from bursting.) Instead of tasting overcooked, they actually develop very deep flavor and a creamy texture.

POTATOES, NEW RED

- Whole, medium (2 ounces each): 7–8 minutes under high pressure
- Whole, small (1 ounce each): 5–6 minutes under high pressure

Scrub the potatoes well; it is not necessary to peel them. Before cooking, pierce them in a few places to prevent the skins from bursting. For best results, halve potatoes that weigh more than 2 ounces.

Whole red potatoes steamed on a rack turn out well, but braising them right in the liquid takes less time and results in better flavor and texture.

POTATOES, SWEET

- Large, quartered: 5–7 minutes under high pressure
- ¼-inch slices: 2–3 minutes under high pressure

Always peel sweet potatoes before pressure-cooking; if you don't they burst open and the flesh disperses. Properly pressure-cooked sweet potatoes are easily pierced with a fork but firm rather than mushy.

RUTABAGA (SWEDE)

- ½-inch dice: 5–6 minutes under high pressure

Peel off the skin, which is usually coated with wax. Properly cooked rutabaga is firm but easily pierced with a fork.

The rutabaga—a rather oversized relative of the turnip—has a distinctively strong flavor that people seem to either hate or love. I stand somewhere in the middle, preferring rutabaga when it is mashed or pureed with another vegetable, such as carrots or potatoes.

SQUASH

- Acorn (about 2 pounds), halves: 6–7 minutes under high pressure
- Butternut, ½-inch slices: 3–4 minutes under high pressure
- Pattypan (about 2 pounds), whole: 10–12 minutes under high pressure
- All peeled winter squash, 1½-inch chunks: 3–4 minutes under high pressure

When serving squash in slices or chunks, cook it for the minimum recommended time. For a puree, cook a minute or two longer.

Peel butternut squash if you're pureeing it; otherwise don't bother, as the pressure cooker softens the skin so much that it becomes good to eat. Cut the squash in half and remove the seeds, then cut each half into ½-inch slices.

Acorn squash is difficult to peel, so it's best to halve it, remove the seeds, and cook it unpeeled. Serve it in the skin, or scoop out the pulp and puree or cut into chunks.

Flat pattypan squash is also difficult to peel. Cook it whole, then cut it in half or quarters, remove the seeds and skin, and serve pureed or in chunks.

TOMATOES

There's no point to steaming plain tomatoes on a rack, but the pressure cooker produces superb sauces in record time. Either remove the skins prior to cooking or pass the cooked sauce through a food mill. I was once too lazy to do either and regretted it; tomato skins are nasty and the "pc" doesn't tenderize them.

TURNIPS

- Medium-large (4 ounces each), quartered: 3–4 minutes under high pressure

- Small, whole (1½ ounces each): 7 minutes under high pressure
- ¼-inch slices: 1–2 minutes under high pressure

Always peel turnips, as their skins are bitter. Properly cooked turnips are firm, but easily pierced with a fork.

ZUCCHINI

- ½-inch slices: 2–3 minutes total cooking time

I was surprised at how nicely zucchini cooks under pressure. I expected waterlogged mush, but instead got crisp, flavorful slices. For a tasty soup, try Pureed Zucchini Soup (page 44).

VEGETABLE COOKING TIMES AT A GLANCE

Since there is considerable variation in how vegetables respond to pressure-steaming, I've come up with a star system to guide you. One star indicates those vegetables that are steamed effectively under pressure. Two stars go to those vegetables that actually improve in flavor and texture with this technique. I don't recommend steaming vegetables that have no stars (unless you intend to puree them), as they tend to cook unevenly or become waterlogged. (A wonderful alternative is to braise them; see page 130.)

Because many people prefer their vegetables slightly crunchy, I have offered a 1- or 2-minute range of cooking time. Use the shorter time if your vegetables are very fresh and you prefer them slightly underdone. For soft-cooked vegetables, especially those that will be pureed, go for the longer cooking time.

Remember: All timing refers to vegetables set on a rack over *boiling* water.

VEGETABLE COOKING TIMES AT A GLANCE
For Steaming Quick-Cooking Vegetables on a Rack Above Water
(See basic guidelines for steaming vegetables, page 170.)

APPROXIMATE MINUTES OF TOTAL COOKING TIME[†]

	0	1	2	3	4	5	6
ASPARAGUS							
* AVERAGE		•	•				
PENCIL		•					
BEANS, GREEN							
* WHOLE			•	•			
* HALVED OR FRENCHED			•	•			

	0	1	2	3	4	5	6
BEET GREENS			•	•			
BROCCOLI							
* LARGE FLORETS			•	•			
* STALKS, PEELED, 1/4-INCH SLICES				•	•		
* STALKS, PEELED, 1/8-INCH SLICES			•	•			
BRUSSELS SPROUTS							
LARGE, 2 INCHES LONG					•	•	
* SMALL, 1 1/2 INCHES LONG				•	•		
CABBAGE							
WHITE OR SAVOY, QUARTERED				•	•		
COARSELY SHREDDED		•					
CAULIFLOWER							
* LARGE FLORETS			•	•			
CELERIAC							
1/2-INCH DICE				•	•		
CELERY							
1-INCH SLICES				•	•		
CORN ON THE COB							
* LARGE, OLD				•	•		
YOUNG, FRESH			•	•			
EGGPLANT							
1 1/2-INCH CHUNKS			•	•			
LEEKS							
WHOLE, LARGE (WHITE PART ONLY)				•	•		
WHOLE, SMALL (WHITE PART ONLY)			•	•			
OKRA							
** SMALL PODS			•	•			
ZUCCHINI							
* 1 1/2-INCH SLICES			•	•			

†The countdown begins the minute the lid is locked into place
*Steams effectively
**Flavor and texture improve with steaming
No stars: Steam only for purees

VEGETABLE COOKING TIMES AT A GLANCE

For Steaming Slower-Cooking Vegetables on a Rack Above Water (See basic guidelines for steaming vegetables, page 170.)

APPROXIMATE MINUTES UNDER HIGH PRESSURE†

	0	1	2	3	4	5	6	7	8	9	10	11	12	13	14	15	16	17	18	19	20	21	22
ARTICHOKES																							
* WHOLE, LARGE (9–10 OUNCES)										•	•	•											
* WHOLE, MEDIUM (6–8 OUNCES)							•	•	•														
* BABY (1 OUNCE EACH)				•	•																		
BEETS																							
* WHOLE, LARGE (5–6 OUNCES)																					•	•	•
** WHOLE, SMALL (3–4 OUNCES)												•	•	•									
* ¹/₄-INCH SLICES				•	•	•																	
CARROTS																							
LARGE WHOLE							•	•	•														
** LARGE, 2-INCH CHUNKS					•	•	•																
LARGE, ¹/₄-INCH SLICES		•																					
CHESTNUTS																							
* FRESH, UNSHELLED						•	•																
* DRIED, PEELED																•							
COLLARD GREENS																							
COARSELY CHOPPED						•	•																
KALE																							
COARSELY CHOPPED		•	•																				
ONIONS																							
* SMALL, WHITE (2 OUNCES)					•	•																	
SMALL, WHITE (¹/₂ OUNCE)			•	•																			

†The countdown begins the minute the lid is locked into place.

Vegetable	Steaming time (minutes)
PARSNIPS	
1-INCH CHUNKS	2, 3, 4
¹/₄-INCH SLICES	1
POTATOES, WHITE	
MEDIUM (5–6 OUNCES), QUARTERED	5, 6, 7
¹/₄-INCH SLICES	3
POTATOES, NEW RED	
* WHOLE, MEDIUM (2 OUNCES)	7, 8
* WHOLE, SMALL (1 OUNCE)	5, 6
POTATOES, SWEET	
* LARGE (7–8 OUNCES), QUARTERED	6, 7
* ¹/₄-INCH SLICES	3
RUTABAGA	
* ¹/₂-INCH DICE	5, 6
SQUASH	
* ACORN, HALVED	6, 7
* BUTTERNUT, ¹/₂-INCH SLICES	4, 5
* PATTYPAN, WHOLE (2 POUNDS)	10, 11, 12
* WINTER, 1¹/₂-INCH CHUNKS	4, 5
TURNIPS	
* MEDIUM (4 OUNCES), QUARTERED	3, 4
* SMALL (1¹/₂ OUNCES), WHOLE	7
* ¹/₄-INCH SLICES	1

Time scale: 0 1 2 3 4 5 6 7 8 9 10 11 12 13 14 15 16 17 18 19 20 21 22

*Steams effectively
**Flavor and texture improve with steaming
No stars: Steam only for purees

Beans

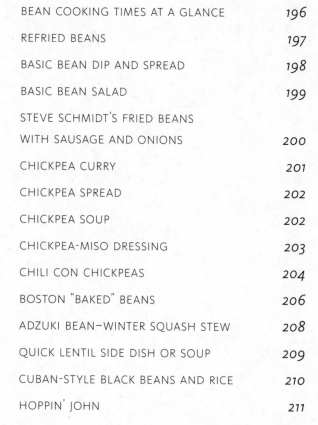

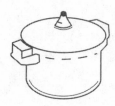
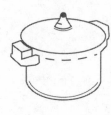

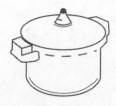

With the current enthusiasm for bistro fare and hearty home-style cooking, beans are finally getting the attention they deserve. And it's a good thing too, since they're one of the best sources of nutrition around: high in protein, fiber, vitamins, and minerals, low in fat (with the exception of soybeans), and completely free of cholesterol. With all of this good news about beans, it's a matter of great good fortune that they are also delicious, filling, and soul-satisfying to eat.

The pressure cooker can produce cooked lentils in 9 minutes and tender chickpeas in the amount of time it takes you to head for the nearest supermarket to buy a can—35 minutes to be precise. And an additional boon: Pressure-cooked beans are ready in a flash with no presoaking.

I love beans, so I'm delighted that I can now prepare them on the spur of the moment. I'm also very enthusiastic about the increased availability of many unusual varieties. Christmas limas, for example, are large, gorgeous, brown-speckled beans that suggest the taste of chestnuts. Scarlet runners are also oversized; they sport brilliant red coats and have a taste and texture reminiscent of potatoes. Both beans are absolutely elegant when served plain, with just a whisper of butter, salt, and pepper.

If you can't locate these and other "boutique" beans locally, they are available by mail order and are well worth the cost—$3 to $5 per pound on average, plus shipping. One excellent source of heirloom beans is Rancho Gordo, *www.ranchogordo.com* (707-259-1935).

Some people avoid eating beans because their feast is followed by an uncomfortable bout of flatulence. This discomfort is caused by gas-producing complex sugars in beans that are not easy to digest.

For many years, it was believed that presoaking beans and tossing away the soaking water reduced these troublesome sugars and the flatulence problem. Since this theory has been proven false, and because those drawn to the pressure cooker want to get dinner on the table quickly, I don't recommend presoaking beans. (I do, however, recommend taking the digestive enzyme sold under the trademarked name of Beano. It is usually quite helpful.)

A FEW RULES TO KEEP IN MIND

**Beans are considered "forbidden foods" by some pressure-cooker manufacturers, since foaming action can push a bean or loose skin into the vent and clog it. Use 4 cups of water and 1 tablespoon of oil (which controls foaming) for each cup of dried beans and you won't experience any difficulty.

***Never add salt or acidic ingredients (such as tomatoes or molasses)* to beans before they are almost entirely cooked. Salt and acids cause the beans' skins to harden, and they won't become tender no matter how long you cook them. (An exception to this general rule can be made when pressure-cooking soups: Adding a small amount of tomatoes or using a lightly salted broth may lengthen cooking time slightly, but does not prevent the beans from softening.)

**Use the natural pressure release when cooking beans. The 10 minutes or so of depressurization gently finishes off the cooking process, resulting in more evenly cooked beans. Using a quick-release method causes turbulence in the pot and causes the beans to burst open and lose their shape.

**In the unlikely event that you hear loud sputtering while cooking beans, place the cooker under cold running water to bring down the pressure. Remove and clean the lid, vent, and rubber gasket. Lock the lid back in place and proceed with cooking.

**Always clean the lid and vent thoroughly after cooking beans.

COOKING TIME

Beans are like snowflakes: No two are alike so it is impossible to give precise cooking times. It's just a fact of life (and beans) that even within a single batch, some will be perfectly cooked while others remain a bit crunchy. This is because of the variations in age and dryness within any given handful.

The good news is that cooking times for most beans are not quite as critical as they are with fresh vegetables. An extra minute is unlikely to turn them to mush. For firm-cooked beans to be used in salads or to be cooked more in soups or stews, check for doneness after the minimum time indicated in the chart. For soft beans that will be pureed or used in refried beans, the longer cooking time works best.

BASIC RULES FOR COOKING BEANS

Pick over beans, rinse, and drain. Cook 1 cup of unsoaked beans with 4 cups of water plus 1 tablespoon of oil. Add 3 cups of water and 1 tablespoon of oil for each additional cup of beans. Beans with the same cooking times may be cooked together, but be prepared for their colors and flavors to mingle.

- Do not fill the cooker above the halfway mark.
- For firm-cooked beans, check for doneness after the minimum time indicated. For soft-cooked beans, use the longer cooking time.
- When the cooking time is up, let the pressure come down naturally. If the beans are not tender, cover (but do not lock)

and simmer until done. If time permits, let the beans cool in the broth.

• Drain the beans, if you wish. If the broth tastes good, reserve it for your next soup or stew.

BEAN COOKING TIMES AT A GLANCE

BEANS (1 CUP DRY)	MINUTES UNDER PRESSURE, THEN NATURAL PRESSURE RELEASE	YIELD IN CUPS
ADZUKI	16–21	2
ANASAZI	20–22	2¼
BLACK (TURTLE)	22–25	2
BLACK-EYED (COW) PEAS	9–11	2¼
CANNELLINI	28–32	2
CHICKPEAS (GARBANZO)	32–35	2½
CHRISTMAS LIMA	16–18	1¾
CRANBERRY	28–34	2¼
FAVA*	22–28	2
FLAGEOLETS	28–34	2
GREAT NORTHERN	25–30	2¼
LENTILS	2–4	2
LIMA (LARGE)**	9–10	2½
LIMA (BABY)	13–15	2½
NAVY (PEA)	22–25	2
PEAS (SPLIT, GREEN)	10–12	2
PEAS (WHOLE, GREEN)	16–18	2
PIGEON PEAS (GANDULES)	20–25	3
PINTO	22–25	2¼
NAVY (PEA)	16–25	2
RED KIDNEY	25–30	2
SCARLET RUNNER	17–20	1½
SOYBEANS (BEIGE)**	28–35	2¼
SOYBEANS (BLACK)**	32–37	2½

*Skins remain leathery after cooking and must be removed before serving unless the beans are pureed
**Require 2 tablespoons of oil for each cup of dried beans

Refried Beans

This Mexican dish is traditionally made with pinto or kidney beans, but any type will work. The trick is to cook the beans until quite soft so they can easily be mashed with the back of a spoon. If your beans are not soft enough for mashing by hand, pulse them a few times in the food processor with about ⅓ cup of the cooking liquid to create a very coarse puree.

Although it's not traditional, I like to zip up the taste of refried beans with a few teaspoons of lime juice stirred in at the end.

Serve them hot, since they become hard when cold. Crumble queso fresco or tangy goat cheese on top, if desired, or serve in a large bowl with tortilla chips or as a vegetable side dish. SERVES 6

2 tablespoons olive oil or bacon drippings

2 teaspoons whole cumin seeds

1 large onion, finely chopped

1 to 2 large garlic cloves, minced

4 cups soft-cooked beans, such as pinto or kidney

Approximately 1 cup bean cooking liquid, vegetable broth, or water

Pinch of ground chipotle pepper

1 to 2 teaspoons freshly squeezed lime juice (optional)

¾ teaspoon salt, or to taste

In a large skillet, heat the oil. Add and sizzle the cumin seeds for 10 seconds while stirring. Add the onion and garlic, and sauté until the onion is soft and lightly browned, 3 to 4 minutes. Reduce the heat to medium, and add about one-third of the cooked beans and ⅓ cup of the liquid, mashing the beans with the back of a spoon—or if the beans are already pureed, stir them into the liquid to create a coarse mash.

While the mixture is simmering and the liquid is being absorbed into the bean puree, continue adding beans and liquid in two more batches. Add the chipotle, lime juice (if desired), and salt. Serve immediately.

Basic Bean Dip and Spread
This zesty spread is good on crackers or as a dip for raw vegetables.

MAKES APPROXIMATELY 2½ CUPS

1 small garlic clove

1 celery stalk, chopped

2 scallions, chopped

2 cups soft-cooked beans (any variety)

1 teaspoon chili powder

2 tablespoons olive oil

1 tablespoon cider vinegar

Dash of ground chipotle pepper (optional)

1 teaspoon dried oregano

1/2 teaspoon salt, or to taste

1/4 cup finely minced fresh parsley or cilantro

2 to 3 tablespoons reserved bean cooking liquid or water

With the motor of the food processor running, pop the garlic clove through the feed tube and chop. Add the celery and scallions and pulse a few times. Add the remaining ingredients and process until smooth, thinning with bean cooking liquid or water as required. Adjust the seasonings before serving.

Basic Bean Salad

Use three different types of beans to make this salad—black beans, pintos, and navy beans are a nice combination—or only one type, such as chickpeas or lentils. The raw vegetables provide texture and color contrast, while the citrus juice and Spanish olives add a piquant contrast to the mellow beans.

Serve warm, at room temperature, or chilled. The salad can be stored in the refrigerator for up to 3 days, but is likely to need a pick-me-up of extra olive oil and lime juice on the second or third day.

SERVES 4–6

3 cups cooked beans
3 scallions, finely chopped
1 green or red bell pepper, seeded and finely diced
2 celery stalks, thinly sliced
2 large carrots, coarsely chopped
1/2 cup finely minced fresh parsley, cilantro, or dill
1/3 cup minced pimiento-stuffed olives
1/4 cup olive oil
1/4 cup freshly squeezed lime or lemon juice
1 tablespoon prepared mustard, preferably coarse Dijon-style
1 teaspoon salt, or to taste
Dash of cayenne pepper (optional)
Garnish: 1/2 cup crumbled queso fresco, goat cheese, or feta cheese
  (optional)

In a large bowl or storage container, toss together the beans, scallions, bell pepper, celery, carrots, parsley, and olives. In a small jar, combine the oil, lime juice, mustard, salt, and cayenne (if using). Shake well to mix and pour over the bean mixture. Toss the salad until the dressing is well distributed. Garnish with queso fresco, if desired. Serve immediately or refrigerate until needed.

Steve Schmidt's Fried Beans with Sausage and Onions
A couldn't-be-simpler, delicious dish made with either hot or sweet sausages.

SERVES 4

2 cups (about 1 pound) fresh sausage meat, casings removed if
  necessary
1 to 2 tablespoons olive oil (optional)
3 cups coarsely chopped onions
4 cups firm-cooked beans (any variety)
Salt and freshly ground black pepper
Garnish: chopped fresh parsley

Crumble the sausage meat into a heavy-bottomed 10- to 12-inch skillet. Cook over moderately high heat, stirring, until the sausage is no longer pink, adding oil if needed to prevent sticking. Add the onions and cook until the onions are lightly browned.

Stir in the beans and continue cooking over moderate heat until hot throughout. Add salt and pepper to taste and garnish with parsley.

Chickpea Curry

Chickpeas cooked under pressure retain their shape beautifully and develop a remarkably creamy texture. Serve this curry as a main dish over rice or as a vegetable side dish. To make it more substantial, after the chickpeas are cooked, stir in 1/4 cup raisins and one 10-ounce package frozen (defrosted) chopped spinach. Heat thoroughly, and adjust the seasonings before serving. SERVES 4

(35 MINUTES UNDER HIGH PRESSURE, THEN 15 MINUTES FOR NATURAL PRESSURE RELEASE)

1 tablespoon oil

1 teaspoon whole cumin seeds

1 cup chopped onion

1 medium red bell pepper, seeded and diced

1 tablespoon mild curry powder

Dash of cayenne pepper (optional)

One 3-inch stick cinnamon, broken in two, or 1/2 teaspoon ground cinnamon

1 1/2 cups dried chickpeas, picked over and rinsed

1 quart (4 cups) water

2 teaspoons freshly grated ginger

1 teaspoon salt, or to taste

Heat the oil in the cooker. Add the cumin seeds and sizzle for 10 seconds. Stir in the onion and red bell pepper and cook for 3 minutes, stirring frequently. Add the curry powder, cayenne (if using), cinnamon, chickpeas, and water.

Lock the lid in place and over high heat bring to high pressure. Adjust the heat to maintain high pressure and cook for 35 minutes. Turn off the heat and allow the pressure to come down naturally, about 15 minutes. Remove the lid, tilting it away from you to allow steam to escape.

If the chickpeas are not sufficiently cooked, replace the lid and simmer over low heat until tender. Discard the cinnamon sticks (if used).

The mixture will thicken on standing, but if you are serving it right away, puree some of the chickpeas and stir the puree into the pot. Add the ginger and salt to taste.

Chickpea Spread
To create a hummuslike spread or dip, puree 1 cup of drained curried chickpeas with 2 to 3 tablespoons of the reserved cooking liquid. **MAKES APPROXIMATELY 1 CUP**

Chickpea Soup
To create a creamy soup, use an immersion blender to puree the chickpeas, adding vegetable broth as needed to reach a desired consistency. If you wish the soup to have some texture, before pureeing remove some whole chickpeas; then stir them back in. **SERVES 4–6**

Chickpea-Miso Dressing
A delightful use for leftover cooked chickpeas, this fat-free dressing is tasty on grains, grain salads, pasta, and steamed vegetables served warm or at room temperature. The dressing thickens upon standing and can be thinned with additional water or chickpea cooking liquid.

MAKES APPROXIMATELY 1½ CUPS

1 cup cooked chickpeas
2 tablespoons miso (see Note)
$1/2$ to 1 cup reserved chickpea cooking liquid or water
$1/4$ cup finely minced fresh parsley
2 teaspoons finely minced fresh ginger
2 scallions, finely chopped
Soy sauce to taste

In a food processor or blender, process all ingredients until smooth, starting with $1/2$ cup chickpea cooking liquid or water; then add more liquid by the tablespoon as needed to reach the desired consistency.

NOTE: Miso, fermented soybean paste, is available in health-food stores. The most flavorful is unpasteurized, which is refrigerated. If unavailable, substitute soy sauce or salt to taste.

Chili con Chickpeas

Here is a delicious vegetarian chili made with chickpeas. For a "meatier" dish, stir in diced cooked ham, sausage, chicken, or pork at the end of cooking. Spoon the chili over rice, millet, or noodles. There's plenty of sauce, so serve it in bowls.

SERVES 6

(35 MINUTES UNDER HIGH PRESSURE, THEN 15 MINUTES FOR NATURAL PRESSURE RELEASE)

2 tablespoons olive oil
1 tablespoon whole cumin seeds
2 to 3 garlic cloves, minced
2 large onions, coarsely chopped
1 large green bell pepper, seeded and coarsely chopped
3 cups water
3 carrots, peeled and cut into 3 to 4 chunks
2 cups dried chickpeas, picked over and rinsed
1 tablespoon chili powder
1 teaspoon dried oregano
Ground chipotle pepper to taste (optional)
One 28-ounce can crushed tomatoes in thick tomato puree
2 medium zucchini, diced
1/2 cup finely minced fresh cilantro
Salt

Heat the oil in the cooker. Add the cumin seeds and sizzle for 10 seconds, stirring constantly. Add the garlic, onions, and green pepper, and sauté until the onions are soft, about 3 minutes.

Stir in the water, carrots, chickpeas, chili powder, oregano, and chipotle (if using). Pour the tomatoes on top. *Do not stir.*

Lock the lid in place and over high heat bring to high pressure. Adjust the heat to maintain high pressure and cook for 35 minutes. Turn off the heat and let the pressure drop naturally, about 15 minutes. Remove the lid, tilting it away from you to allow steam to escape.

If the chickpeas are not close to tender, cover and simmer as required. Add the zucchini. Cover and cook over medium heat until the chickpeas and zucchini are tender, about 10 minutes. If you wish to thicken the stew, puree some of the chickpeas and stir them back in. Stir in the cilantro and salt to taste. Adjust the seasonings and serve.

Boston "Baked" Beans

This dish has much of the flavor of Boston baked beans, without the 3 hours of simmering. The beans are precooked in the pressure cooker for 15 minutes before the skin-hardening molasses, tomato paste, and mustard are added.

Since dried beans absorb varying degrees of water and the cooking liquid thickens considerably upon standing, you may either need to thin this mixture with a bit of water or drain off some of the liquid at the end of cooking. Make this adjustment before adding the vinegar and correcting the seasonings.

Try adding some fried sausages or grilled frankfurters to the beans for a hearty entrée.

SERVES 6

(16 MINUTES UNDER HIGH PRESSURE, THEN 15 MINUTES FOR NATURAL PRESSURE RELEASE)

1¹/₂ cups dried navy beans, picked over and rinsed

2 bay leaves

1¹/₂ quarts (6 cups) water

2 tablespoons oil, divided

1 large onion, coarsely chopped

2 large garlic cloves, minced

¹/₄ cup molasses

¹/₄ cup Dijon-style mustard

¹/₄ cup tomato paste

4 whole cloves

One 3-inch stick cinnamon, broken in two

1 to 3 teaspoons cider vinegar

1 teaspoon salt, or to taste

Place the beans, bay leaves, water, and 1 tablespoon oil in the cooker. Lock the lid in place and over high heat bring to high pressure. Adjust the heat to maintain high pressure and cook for 15 minutes. Reduce the pressure by placing the cooker under cold running water. Remove the lid, tilting it away from you to allow steam to escape. Drain the beans, reserving the liquid. Return the beans and 2 cups of liquid to the cooker. Discard any remaining liquid or reserve it for making your next soup.

Heat the remaining tablespoon of oil in a skillet. Sauté the onions and garlic until the onions begin to brown around the edges, 3 to 4 minutes. Stir in the molasses, mustard, tomato paste, cloves, and cinnamon. Pour the mixture on top of the beans. *Do not stir.*

Lock the lid in place and over high heat return to high pressure. Adjust the heat to maintain high pressure and cook for an additional 10 minutes. Allow the pressure to come down naturally, about 15 minutes. Remove the lid, tilting it away from you to allow steam to escape. If the beans are not tender, replace (but do not lock) the lid and simmer until done.

Before serving, remove the cloves, bay leaves, and cinnamon sticks. The mixture will thicken on standing, but if you wish to thicken it immediately, puree some of the beans and stir the puree back in. Stir in the vinegar and salt.

Adzuki Bean–Winter Squash Stew

The bright orange of the squash and the crimson color of adzuki beans make this quite a beautiful dish. If you like, substitute the more readily available kidney beans for an equally dramatic effect. The beans get a 14-minute head start before the quick-cooking squash is added. Serve over noodles or rice to absorb the abundant sauce.　　SERVES 4–6

(18 MINUTES UNDER HIGH PRESSURE)

1 cup dried adzuki beans, picked over and rinsed

3 cups water or vegetable broth

1 tablespoon oil

1 to 2 teaspoons ground ginger

1/2 teaspoon ground cinnamon

2 pounds butternut squash, peeled and cut into 1 1/2-inch chunks

1/2 pound parsnips, preferably small, peeled and cut into 1/2-inch slices

1 to 2 tablespoons unsalted butter

Salt

Place the beans, water, and oil in the cooker. Lock the lid in place and over high heat bring to high pressure. Adjust the heat to maintain high pressure and cook for 14 minutes. Reduce the pressure with a quick-release method. Remove the lid, tilting it away from you to allow steam to escape.

Stir in the ginger to taste, cinnamon, squash, and parsnips. Lock the lid in place and over high heat return to high pressure. Adjust the heat to maintain high pressure and cook for an additional 4 minutes. Reduce the pressure with a quick-release method. Remove the lid, tilting it away from you to allow steam to escape.

If the beans are not tender, replace (but do not lock) the lid and simmer until done. Stir in butter and salt to taste.

Quick Lentil Side Dish or Soup   *Mustard*

and parsley stirred into lentils elevate them to a high status in a matter of seconds. Drain and serve in small bowls for an unusual side dish, or serve in their cooking liquid for a delicious soup.   SERVES 2–3

(10 MINUTES UNDER HIGH PRESSURE)

2 cups dried lentils, picked over and rinsed
1 bay leaf
1 to 2 large garlic cloves, minced
1 large onion, coarsely chopped
1 tablespoon oil
1½ quarts (6 cups) water
2 to 3 tablespoons prepared mustard, preferably Dijon-style
¼ cup finely minced fresh parsley
1 teaspoon salt, or to taste

Combine the lentils, bay leaf, garlic, onion, oil, and water in the cooker. Lock the lid in place and over high heat bring to high pressure. Adjust the heat to maintain high pressure and cook for 10 minutes. Reduce the pressure with a quick-release method. Remove the lid, tilting it away from you to allow steam to escape.

If the lentils are not done, replace (but do not lock) the lid in place and simmer until done.

Remove the bay leaf. If using as a side dish, drain off most of the cooking liquid. Stir in the mustard, parsley, and salt. Adjust the seasonings and serve.

Cuban-Style Black Beans and Rice

My twist on this classic combination is to toss in olives and cilantro just before serving. This recipe calls for cooked black beans. SERVES 4–6

(5 MINUTES UNDER HIGH PRESSURE, THEN 5 MINUTES FOR
NATURAL PRESSURE RELEASE)

2 tablespoons olive oil

1 large onion, coarsely chopped

2 to 3 garlic cloves, minced

1 green bell pepper, seeded and coarsely chopped

1 cup uncooked extra long-grain white rice

1^3/$_4$ cups water

1 teaspoon salt, or to taste

1 bay leaf

Generous dash of crushed red pepper flakes or cayenne pepper
   (optional)

^{1}/$_2$ teaspoon dried thyme

One 14-ounce can tomatoes, coarsely chopped, including juice

2 cups cooked black beans

^{1}/$_4$ cup chopped fresh cilantro

^{1}/$_3$ cup minced pimiento-stuffed olives

Heat the oil in the cooker. Sauté the onions, garlic, and green pepper until the onions are soft, about 3 minutes. Stir in the rice and coat it well with the oil. Add the water, salt, bay leaf, crushed red pepper, and thyme. Pour the tomatoes on top. *Do not stir.*

Lock the lid in place and over high heat bring to high pressure. Adjust the heat to maintain high pressure and cook for 5 minutes. Let the pressure drop naturally for 5 minutes, then quick-release any pressure remaining in the cooker. Remove the lid, tilting it away from you to allow steam to escape.

If the rice is not evenly tender, stir well. Set the lid in place and steam in the residual heat for another few minutes. Remove the bay leaf and stir in the beans, cilantro, and olives. Adjust the seasonings and serve.

Hoppin' John

Traditionally served on New Year's Day, this southern combination of black-eyed peas and rice is said to bring good luck. The rice and beans are cooked separately and stirred together just before serving. For a more dramatic flavor, cook the peas with a smoked ham hock.

SERVES 6

(5 MINUTES UNDER HIGH PRESSURE, THEN 5 MINUTES FOR NATURAL PRESSURE RELEASE)

2 tablespoons bacon drippings or olive oil

1 large onion, coarsely chopped

1 large garlic clove, minced

1 small green bell pepper, seeded and chopped

1 cup uncooked extra long-grain white rice

2 cups water

1 bay leaf

2 tablespoons tomato paste

3/4 teaspoon salt, or to taste

2 cups cooked black-eyed peas

Freshly ground black pepper and Tabasco sauce

Heat the bacon drippings or oil in the cooker. Sauté the onion, garlic, and green pepper until the onion is soft, about 3 minutes. Stir in the rice and coat it well with the oil. Add the water, bay leaf, tomato paste, and salt.

Lock the lid in place and over high heat bring to high pressure. Adjust the heat to maintain high pressure and cook for 5 minutes. Let the pressure drop naturally for 5 minutes, then quick-release any pressure remaining in the cooker. Remove the lid, tilting it away from you to allow steam to escape.

Remove the bay leaf, and stir in the peas, pepper, and Tabasco sauce to taste. Adjust the seasonings and serve.

Rice, Risotto, and Other Grains

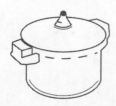

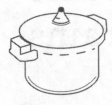

Cooking rice under pressure saves time and produces a tasty product with a pleasantly chewy texture. White rice takes only 10 minutes; brown rice is done to perfection in less than 30. Perhaps most exciting of all is the good news for risotto lovers: The pressure cooker creates superb results in 4 minutes under pressure followed by just a few minutes of stirring to finish the dish off. See page 228 for details.

For the same reason that the pressure cooker makes such superb risotto—it yanks the starch right out of the rice—it produces a slightly sticky rice. This characteristic is more exaggerated with brown rice, which requires a longer cooking time than white.

Although I'd always preferred rice with nicely separated grains, much to my surprise I've grown accustomed to pressure-cooked rice and now actually like it better. Try it and see what you think.

Thanks to the pressure cooker, whole grains other than brown rice can also be prepared on a whim, in dramatically less time than is normally required. Barley is done in only 18 minutes, and wheat berries (whole-grain wheat), which normally take 2 to 3 hours to cook, can be on your table in 35 minutes with no presoaking.

Growing interest in whole-grain cooking has brought a wide range of exotic grains into America's kitchens. From South America come delicate quinoa and amaranth. Southeast Asia is the source of hearty, chewy Job's Tears. All of these grains are delicious, offering your taste buds a great treat and your body a good boost of nutrition. If you can't find them in your supermarket, they'll be readily available in any well-stocked health-food store.

COOKING RICE

To control foaming action when the rice is cooking, always add 1 tablespoon of butter or oil. The amount of liquid required varies slightly from one type of cooker to another. Begin by following my basic recipes; if your rice is not done by the time that all of the liquid is absorbed, begin your next batch with a few additional tablespoons of water. Experiment in this way until you come up with the best formula for your cooker and taste.

FLAVORING OPTIONS

When preparing rice to serve with Italian, French, Spanish, or American Southern food, consider substituting beef, chicken, or vegetable broth for the water and adding one or more of the following per 1 cup of dry rice:

1 large garlic clove, minced
1 bay leaf
1/2 teaspoon dried oregano, basil, or thyme
Dash of cayenne pepper
1/2 teaspoon sweet Hungarian paprika or smoked Spanish paprika
Olive oil instead of unsalted butter or other vegetable oil

When serving rice with Indian, Moroccan, or Middle Eastern food, consider substituting orange or apple juice for half of the water and adding one or more of the following per 1 cup of dry rice:

One 3-inch stick cinnamon, broken in two
2 to 3 crushed cardamom pods or 1/4 teaspoon ground cardamom
1/4 teaspoon ground coriander
1 to 2 teaspoons curry powder
2 to 3 whole cloves or 1/8 teaspoon ground cloves
1/8 teaspoon ground allspice
2 to 3 quarter-sized slices fresh ginger or 1/4 teaspoon ground
    ginger

Pinch of saffron or $1/4$ teaspoon ground turmeric

$1/4$ cup toasted pine nuts

$1/3$ cup raisins, currants, or chopped apricots or prunes

$1/3$ cup grated unsweetened coconut, preferably toasted

I generally add half of the normally recommended amount of salt to white rice and find it quite sufficient. I rarely add any salt at all to plain-cooked brown rice since it masks the grains' natural sweetness.

Basic White Rice

For a moist rice, use 1³/4 cups liquid. For a drier rice, use 1¹/2 cups.

MAKES 3 CUPS COOKED RICE

(3 MINUTES UNDER HIGH PRESSURE, THEN 7 MINUTES FOR
NATURAL PRESSURE RELEASE)

1 cup extra long-grain white rice

1¹/2 to 1³/4 cups water, broth, or bouillon

1 tablespoon oil or unsalted butter, cut into bits

¹/2 teaspoon salt, or to taste (less if using canned broth or bouillon)

Additional flavorings as desired (see page 216)

Combine the ingredients in the cooker. Turn the heat to high and stir a few times to blend. Lock the lid in place and over high heat bring to high pressure. Adjust the heat to maintain high pressure and cook for 3 minutes. Turn off the heat and let the pressure drop naturally for 7 minutes. Quick-release any remaining pressure. Remove the lid, tilting it away from you to allow steam to escape.

Taste the rice. If it is not quite done, replace the lid and steam in the residual heat for a few more minutes. When the rice is done, fluff with a fork, adjust the seasonings, and serve.

WHITE RICE COOKING CHART

FOR A DRY RICE, USE THE SMALLER AMOUNT OF LIQUID. FOR A MOIST RICE, USE THE MAXIMUM.

EXTRA LONG-GRAIN WHITE RICE	CUPS LIQUID	OPTIONAL SALT	OIL/BUTTER	YIELD IN CUPS
1 CUP	1¹/2–1³/4	¹/2 T	1 T	3
1¹/2 CUPS	2¹/4–2¹/2	³/4 T	1 T	4–4¹/2
2 CUPS	3–3¹/4	1 T	2 T	5¹/2–6
3 CUPS	4¹/4–4¹/2	1¹/2 T	2¹/2 T	7¹/2–8

Do not cook more than 3 cups of dry white rice in a 6-quart cooker.

Caserole Steamed Rice

Here is a handy way to prepare a small quantity of rice in a heatproof 4- or 5-cup bowl. I use a 5-cup soufflé dish, which I bring right to the table. Before cooking, add any spices and dried herbs you like (see page 216 for suggestions). After cooking, it's nice to toss in some chopped fresh herbs or garnish the rice with toasted pine nuts or sunflower seeds.

MAKES 3 CUPS COOKED RICE

(5 MINUTES UNDER HIGH PRESSURE, THEN 7–10 MINUTES FOR
NATURAL PRESSURE RELEASE)

1 cup extra long-grain white rice
1^1/$_2$ cups water
^{1}/$_2$ teaspoon salt, or to taste
1 tablespoon unsalted butter, cut into bits (optional)

Set the rack in the bottom of the cooker and pour in 2 cups of water. Cut a piece of aluminum foil 1 foot wide by 2 feet long and fold it twice lengthwise to create a long strip about 3 inches wide for lowering the bowl into the cooker.

Combine the rice, water, and salt in a 4- or 5-cup heatproof bowl. Center the bowl on the strip and lower it into the cooker. Loosely fold the ends of the foil strip over the top of the bowl.

Lock the lid in place and over high heat bring to high pressure. Adjust the heat to maintain high pressure and cook for 5 minutes. Let the pressure drop naturally, 7 to 10 minutes. Remove the lid, tilting it away from you to allow steam to escape.

Carefully lift out the bowl with the aid of the foil strips. Stir in the butter (if using) with a fork at the same time as you are fluffing up the rice.

Fragrant Coconut Rice

Serve this aromatic rice alongside one of the pressure-cooked lamb stews, particularly the curry or tagine. The complex flavors belie the ease of preparation. SERVES 4

(3 MINUTES UNDER HIGH PRESSURE, THEN 7 MINUTES FOR
NATURAL PRESSURE RELEASE)

2 tablespoons unsalted butter or oil

1 cup uncooked extra long-grain white rice

1/2 cup unsweetened flaked (or grated) coconut

2 1/4 cups water

1/4 cup dried currants

1/2 teaspoon ground cinnamon

1 teaspoon aniseeds

1/8 teaspoon ground cloves

3/4 teaspoon salt, or to taste

Heat the butter in the cooker. Stir in the rice, coating well with the fat. Add the coconut, water, currants, spices, and salt.

Lock the lid in place and over high heat bring to high pressure. Adjust the heat to maintain high pressure and cook for 3 minutes. Turn off the heat and let the pressure drop naturally for 7 minutes. Quick-release any remaining pressure. Remove the lid, tilting it away from you to allow steam to escape.

Taste the rice. If it is not quite done, replace the lid and steam in the residual heat for a few more minutes. When the rice is done, fluff with a fork, taking care to distribute the spices. Adjust the seasonings and serve.

NOTE: For additional recipes using white rice, check the index under Risotto, Cuban-Style Black Beans and Rice, Hoppin' John, and Rice Pudding.

Basic Brown Rice

I'm crazy about the earthy flavor and delicate sweetness of brown rice and find that with preparation time cut down to 25 minutes, I can make it a frequent part of my dinner menu.

To avoid foaming and to reduce the possibility of rice sticking to the bottom of the cooker, sauté the rice briefly in a tablespoon of butter or oil before adding the boiling water. This gentle toasting also enhances the flavor and prevents the rice from clumping together.

For rice with a distinctly chewy texture, opt for the short-grain variety. It is also less fussy to prepare: You can let the pressure drop naturally and leave the lid on the pot for 5 to 10 additional minutes without damaging the texture. Don't try this casual approach with other types of brown rice or you might find yourself with a sticky mess.

This basic recipe also works with brown basmati and wehani rice.

MAKES 2½–3 CUPS COOKED RICE

(15 MINUTES UNDER HIGH PRESSURE, THEN 10 MINUTES FOR NATURAL PRESSURE RELEASE)

1 tablespoon oil
1 cup short- or long-grain brown rice, picked over, rinsed, and
    drained
1³/₄ cups boiling water, broth, or bouillon
Flavoring options (see page 216)
1/2 teaspoon salt, or to taste (optional)

Heat the oil in the cooker. Sauté the rice until lightly browned, stirring frequently, 1 to 2 minutes. Turn off the heat and stir in the boiling water (watch for sputtering oil), flavoring options, and salt, if using.

Lock the lid in place and over high heat bring to high pressure. Adjust the heat to maintain high pressure and cook for 15 minutes. Turn off the heat and let the pressure drop naturally while the rice steams in the residual heat for 10 minutes. Reduce any remaining pressure with a quick-release method. Remove the lid, tilting it away from you to allow steam to escape.

If the rice is not sufficiently cooked, stir in a few tablespoons of boiling water if the mixture seems dry and replace the lid. Simmer over *very low heat* for another minute or two, or until done. Fluff with a fork and serve immediately.

BROWN RICE COOKING CHART

BROWN RICE	CUPS BOILING LIQUID	OPTIONAL SALT	OIL	APPROXIMATE YIELD IN CUPS
1 CUP	1³/₄	¹/₂ T	1 T	2¹/₄
1¹/₂ CUPS	2¹/₂	³/₄ T	1 T	3¹/₂
2 CUPS	3¹/₂	1 T	1¹/₂ T	5
3 CUPS	5	1¹/₂ T	2 T	7
4 CUPS	6¹/₂	2 T	2 T	10

Do not fill the cooker beyond the halfway mark. Cook under high pressure for 15 minutes. Let the pressure drop naturally for at least 10 minutes.

Carefree Brown Rice

Use this method if you are in a real hurry or are experiencing sticking when you use the basic recipe above. Combine 1¹/₂ cups of brown rice with 5¹/₂ cups of water and 1 tablespoon of oil. Cook under pressure for 15 minutes. Quick-release the pressure by setting the cooker under cold running water. Drain the rice thoroughly. MAKES 3¹/₄ CUPS COOKED RICE

Quick Skillet-Fried Rice or Barley

A quick and healthful dinner, especially when prepared with brown rice.
For a vegetarian version, substitute cubed, firm tofu for the diced ham.

SERVES 3–4

1 tablespoon oil
2 to 3 teaspoons minced fresh ginger
1 to 2 garlic cloves, minced
1 small green or red bell pepper, seeded and chopped
1 cup sliced celery or canned, drained water chestnuts
1/4 pound mushrooms, sliced
3 scallions, white and green parts chopped separately
1/2 pound bean sprouts, well drained
3 cups cooked white or brown rice or pearl barley
1 cup diced, cooked country ham
2 to 3 teaspoons toasted (Asian) sesame oil
1 to 2 tablespoons soy sauce, preferably Japanese shoyu or tamari

In a large skillet, heat the oil. Sauté the ginger and garlic for 30 seconds. Add the bell pepper, celery, mushrooms, and the whites of the scallions, and sauté an additional 2 minutes, stirring frequently.

Stir in the bean sprouts, rice, and ham, and cook over medium heat until the ingredients are hot and most of the liquid given off by the vegetables has evaporated.

Stir in the scallion greens, and season with sesame oil and soy sauce to taste.

NOTE: For other recipes using cooked rice, see Grain Salad with Marinated Artichoke Hearts and Sun-dried Tomatoes (page 241) and Grain Salad with Soy-Lime Vinaigrette (page 242).

Brown Rice with Chestnuts, Prunes, and Apricots

A slightly sweet dish that goes well with roast turkey or baked ham. You can replace the fresh chestnuts with dried chestnuts that have been soaked overnight in ample water to cover.

SERVES 6

(15 MINUTES UNDER HIGH PRESSURE, THEN 10 MINUTES FOR NATURAL PRESSURE RELEASE)

12 fresh chestnuts (about 10 ounces)

2 tablespoons butter or oil

2 celery stalks, thinly sliced

2 large carrots, scrubbed and coarsely chopped

1^1/$_2$ cups uncooked long- or short-grain brown rice, picked over and rinsed

1/3 cup pitted prunes, halved

1/3 cup chopped apricots

1/2 teaspoon ground cinnamon

2^3/$_4$ to 3 cups boiling vegetable or chicken broth or bouillon or water

1 bay leaf

1 teaspoon salt, or to taste (less if using canned broth or bouillon)

2 teaspoons grated orange zest

With a sharp paring knife, make a small "x" in the skin on the flat side of each chestnut. Bring 2 quarts water to a boil in the cooker and cook the chestnuts, uncovered, for 3 minutes. Turn off the heat and lift a few chestnuts at a time from the water with a slotted spoon. Run under cold water to cool, and remove both the peel and the thin skin surrounding each chestnut. If any chestnuts don't peel easily, set them back in the hot water for a few minutes. When done, rinse out the cooker and dry thoroughly.

Heat the butter in the cooker. Sauté the celery and carrots for 2 minutes, then stir in the rice and coat well with the fat. Stir in the chestnuts, prunes, apricots, cinnamon, 2^3/$_4$ cups boiling broth, bay leaf, and salt.

Lock the lid in place and over high heat bring to high pressure. Ad-

just the heat to maintain high pressure and cook for 15 minutes. Let the pressure drop naturally for 10 minutes. Reduce any remaining pressure with a quick-release method. Remove the lid, tilting it away from you to allow steam to escape.

If the rice is not sufficiently cooked, stir in $1/4$ cup additional boiling broth or water if the mixture seems dry, cover, and simmer over low heat for a few more minutes. When the rice is done, remove the bay leaf and stir in the orange zest. Adjust the seasonings before serving.

Brown Rice and Lentil Stew

This recipe calls for short-grain brown rice, which has a delightfully chewy texture—a nice contrast to the pliant lentils.

SERVES 6–8

(15 MINUTES UNDER HIGH PRESSURE, THEN 10 MINUTES FOR NATURAL PRESSURE RELEASE)

2 tablespoons olive oil

3 large garlic cloves, minced

2 cups coarsely chopped onions

3 celery stalks, sliced

2 1/2 cups uncooked short-grain brown rice, picked over and rinsed

3/4 cup dried lentils, picked over and rinsed

1/2 pound mushrooms, sliced

4 3/4 cups chicken or vegetable broth or bouillon

2 bay leaves

1 1/2 teaspoons dried oregano

1 tablespoon prepared mustard

1 cup tomato sauce

Salt

1/2 cup minced fresh parsley

Heat the oil in the cooker. Sauté the garlic and onions until the onions are lightly browned, 4 to 5 minutes. Stir in the celery, brown rice, and lentils, and sauté another minute. Add the mushrooms, broth, bay leaves, oregano, and mustard, and bring to a boil.

Lock the lid in place and over high heat bring to high pressure. Adjust the heat to maintain high pressure and cook for 15 minutes. Let the pressure drop naturally for 10 minutes. Quick-release any remaining pressure. Remove the lid, tilting it away from you to allow steam to escape.

Remove the bay leaves and stir in the tomato sauce, salt to taste, and parsley. If the rice or lentils are not quite done, cover and simmer over low heat until desired consistency, stirring in a bit of boiling water if the mixture seems dry. Adjust the seasonings and serve.

Savory Wild Rice

Wild rice varies dramatically in the amount of time it takes to "butterfly," the term used to describe the grains when they have burst open. I've prepared batches that have been done in 22 minutes, and others that I've had to bring back up to pressure as many as three times before they were the right consistency. Most people agree that taste rewards patience where wild rice is concerned. SERVES 4

(22–30 MINUTES UNDER HIGH PRESSURE)

2 tablespoons unsalted butter
1 medium onion, coarsely chopped
1 cup wild rice, rinsed and drained
2 celery stalks, thinly sliced
3 cups beef, chicken, or vegetable broth or bouillon
1/3 cup loosely packed dried mushrooms (1/2 ounce)
1 bay leaf
3/4 teaspoon salt (less if using canned broth or bouillon)
Freshly ground black pepper
Garnish: 1/4 cup toasted pignoli nuts (optional)

Heat the butter in the cooker. Sauté the onion until soft, about 3 minutes. Stir in the wild rice, taking care to coat the grains with the butter. Stir in the celery, broth, mushrooms, bay leaf, and salt and pepper to taste.

Lock the lid in place and over high heat bring to high pressure. Adjust the heat to maintain high pressure and cook for 22 minutes. Reduce the pressure with a quick-release method. Remove the lid, tilting it away from you to allow steam to escape.

If most or all of the rice has not butterflied, lock the lid back into place and return to high pressure for an additional 2 to 8 minutes, as required. When the rice is done, remove the bay leaf and adjust the seasonings. If the mixture is soupy, use a slotted spoon to transfer the rice to a serving bowl. Garnish with pignoli nuts, if desired.

RISOTTO

I've had many a fine risotto in my day, and I think the ones that emerge from the pressure cooker are among the best. They require little fuss to prepare and nary a stir while cooking under pressure—just set the timer for 4 minutes and have a quick visit with your guests. Then stir for the final few minutes to finish cooking.

For best taste and texture, it's essential to use an Italian short-grain white rice such as Arborio, Carnaroli, or Vialone Nano. In the recipes that follow, I have specified Arborio, since it is readily available in most gourmet and specialty food shops. Traditionally the rice is not rinsed before cooking, as the water would wash away starches that contribute to the velvety sauce enveloping each cooked grain. The perfect risotto should be slightly soupy and properly chewy, with the rice offering just a pleasant resistance to the bite. For this reason, the pressure is always quick-released and the risotto must be served as soon as it is finished.

If the truth be told, I love risotto so much that I often eat leftovers straight from the fridge. The texture is somewhat less than ideal, but the taste is still delicious. Leftover risotto can also be shaped into pancakes and warmed or panfried in a little butter, or heated in the microwave.

Here are a few of my favorite variations. Using the basic formula of 3½ to 4 cups of liquid to 1½ cups of Arborio rice, you can create your own recipes, and if you'd like dozens of traditional and imaginative ideas, have a look at *Risotto* by Judith Barrett and Norma Wasserman. The first three recipes were inspired by suggested combinations in that book. Although classic risottos usually contain wine, I have found the first three versions extremely flavorful without it.

Salt and Risotto

In the recipes that follow, many of the salty ingredients, such as the broth and Parmesan cheese, make it unnecessary to add extra salt.

Add salt to taste after the risotto is cooked and all ingredients have been stirred in.

When I don't have homemade broth on hand, I use Morga Instant Vegetable Broth Mix (available in health-food stores) or Pacific brand chicken broth with excellent results. If you're using a salted canned broth or bouillon, dilute with ⅓ cup of water per cup of broth to avoid excessive saltiness in the risotto.

Risotto with Gruyère and Parmesan

A simple risotto, with ingredients easy to keep on hand for an impromptu meal. Serve with a tossed salad.

SERVES 6 AS AN APPETIZER, 4 AS A MAIN COURSE

(4 MINUTES UNDER HIGH PRESSURE, THEN 3–5 MINUTES FOR EXTRA COOKING)

2 tablespoons unsalted butter

1 tablespoon olive oil

^{1}/3 cup minced onions

1^1/2 cups Arborio rice

3^1/2 to 4 cups vegetable or chicken broth or bouillon

1 cup grated Gruyère (4 ounces)

^{1}/4 cup grated Parmesan

Salt (optional)

3 tablespoons minced fresh parsley

Heat the butter and oil in the cooker. Sauté the onions until soft but not browned, about 2 minutes. Stir in the rice, making sure to coat it thoroughly with the fat. Stir in 3^1/2 cups of the broth (watch for sputtering oil).

Lock the lid in place and over high heat bring to high pressure. Adjust the heat to maintain high pressure and cook for 4 minutes. Reduce the pressure with a quick-release method. Remove the lid, tilting it away from you to allow steam to escape.

The risotto will be fairly soupy at this point. Set the cooker over medium-high heat and boil uncovered, stirring vigorously every minute, until the mixture thickens and the rice is tender but still chewy, 3 to 5 minutes. Add a bit more broth if the mixture becomes dry before the rice reaches the desired consistency. Turn off the heat, stir in the Gruyère and Parmesan, and add salt to taste, if desired. Stir in the parsley and serve immediately.

Risotto with Sun-dried Tomatoes and Smoked Mozzarella *I'm very partial to this simple but intensely flavored combination, and I think you will be too.*

SERVES 6 AS AN APPETIZER, 4 AS A MAIN COURSE

(4 MINUTES UNDER HIGH PRESSURE, THEN 3–5 MINUTES FOR EXTRA COOKING)

1 tablespoon unsalted butter

1 tablespoon oil from sun-dried tomatoes

$1/2$ cup finely minced onion

$1^1/2$ cups Arborio rice

$3^1/2$ to 4 cups vegetable broth or bouillon

$1/3$ cup sun-dried tomatoes, packed in oil, drained and coarsely chopped

1 cup tightly packed, grated smoked mozzarella (5 ounces)

Salt (optional)

$1/4$ cup chopped fresh basil (optional)

Heat the butter and oil in the cooker. Sauté the onion until soft but not browned, about 2 minutes. Stir in the rice, making sure to coat it thoroughly with the fat. Stir in $3^1/2$ cups of the broth (watch for sputtering oil).

Lock the lid in place and over high heat bring to high pressure. Adjust the heat to maintain high pressure and cook for 4 minutes. Reduce the pressure with a quick-release method. Remove the lid, tilting it away from you to allow steam to escape.

The risotto will be fairly soupy at this point. Set the cooker over medium-high heat and boil uncovered, stirring vigorously every minute, until the mixture thickens and the rice is tender but still chewy, 3 to 5 minutes. Add a bit more broth if the mixture becomes dry before the rice reaches the desired consistency. Turn off the heat, and stir in the tomatoes and mozzarella. Add salt to taste and basil (if desired). Serve immediately.

Risotto with Mushrooms, Olives, and Leeks

As far as I'm concerned, the marriage of mushrooms and leeks was made in heaven. Throw in olives and you have a gastronomic ménage à trois that defies description.

SERVES 6 AS AN APPETIZER, 4 AS A MAIN COURSE

(4 MINUTES UNDER HIGH PRESSURE, THEN 3–5 MINUTES FOR EXTRA COOKING)

1 tablespoon unsalted butter

1 tablespoon olive oil

2 medium leeks, white part only, thoroughly rinsed and thinly sliced (about 1 1/2 cups)

1 1/2 cups Arborio rice

1/2 pound mushrooms, stems reserved for another use, caps thinly sliced

1/4 cup pitted, minced black olives, preferably oil-cured

3 1/4 to 3 1/2 cups vegetable or chicken broth or bouillon

1/3 to 1/2 cup grated Parmesan

Salt (optional)

Heat the butter and oil in the cooker. Sauté the leeks until soft but not browned, about 2 minutes. Stir in the rice, making sure to coat it thoroughly with the fat. Stir in the mushrooms, olives, and 3 1/4 cups of the broth (watch for sputtering oil).

Lock the lid in place and over high heat bring to high pressure. Adjust the heat to maintain high pressure and cook for 4 minutes. Reduce the pressure with a quick-release method. Remove the lid, tilting it away from you to allow steam to escape.

The risotto will be fairly soupy at this point. Set the cooker over medium-high heat and boil uncovered, stirring vigorously every minute, until the mixture thickens and the rice is tender but still chewy, 3 to 5 minutes. Add a bit more broth if the mixture becomes dry before the rice reaches the desired consistency. Turn off the heat, stir in the Parmesan, and add salt to taste (if desired). Serve immediately.

Seafood Risotto

Rice is an ideal foil for the variety of seafood in this elegant risotto. Although Parmesan isn't traditionally served with fish in Italy. I think it's delicious here.

SERVES 6 AS AN APPETIZER, 4 AS A MAIN COURSE

(4 MINUTES UNDER HIGH PRESSURE, THEN 3–5 MINUTES FOR EXTRA COOKING)

1 pound mussels, scrubbed and debearded
1 cup dry white or red wine, preferably Italian
3/4 cup water
1 garlic clove, peeled and halved
1/2 pound small shrimp, shelled and deveined
1/2 pound scallops (see Note)
One bottle (8 fluid ounces) clam juice
1 tablespoon olive oil
1 tablespoon unsalted butter
1/2 cup finely minced onion
1/2 teaspoon dried thyme or dried oregano
1 1/2 cups Arborio rice
2 tablespoons minced fresh parsley
1/3 to 1/2 cup grated Parmesan
Salt (optional)

Place the mussels, wine, water, and garlic in the cooker, and set (but do not lock) the lid in place. Steam over high heat until the mussel shells open, 3 to 4 minutes. Remove the mussels to a platter with a slotted spoon, and add the shrimp to the liquid in the cooker. Cook over medium heat while stirring for 30 seconds. Add the scallops and cook an additional 30 seconds. Remove the shrimp and scallops with a slotted spoon and set on another platter. Once the mussels have cooled slightly, remove and discard the shells. Place the mussels with the cooked shrimps and scallops. Cover the platter loosely with aluminum foil and set aside.

Leaving behind any sediment that has fallen to the bottom of the cooker, carefully pour the cooking liquid into a large measuring cup.

Pour in the clam juice and enough water to equal 3½ cups liquid. Set aside.

Rinse and thoroughly dry the cooker. Heat the oil and butter in the cooker. Sauté the onion, stirring frequently, until soft but not browned, about 2 minutes. Stir in the thyme and rice, making sure to coat the rice thoroughly with the fat. (The risotto can be prepared up to this point and left to sit in the pot until shortly before needed.)

About 10 minutes before serving the risotto, stir in the reserved 3½ cups of liquid. (Watch for sputtering if the oil is hot.)

Lock the lid in place and over high heat bring to high pressure. Adjust the heat to maintain high pressure and cook for 4 minutes. Reduce the pressure with a quick-release method. Remove the lid, tilting it away from you to allow steam to escape.

The risotto will be fairly soupy at this point. Set the cooker over medium-high heat and boil uncovered, stirring vigorously every minute, until the mixture thickens and the rice is tender but still chewy, 3 to 5 minutes. Add a bit more broth if the mixture becomes dry before the rice reaches the desired consistency. Turn off the heat, and stir in the parsley, Parmesan, and cooked seafood. Add salt to taste (if desired) and serve immediately.

NOTE: If using sea scallops, cut them into ½-inch dice. Bay scallops can be cooked as is.

Barley Risotto

A hearty and economical alternative to risotto made with Arborio rice, barley risotto has become a favorite standby when I yearn for something simple and filling.

Depending upon my mood, I stir in blue cheese, which is assertive in flavor and adds a wonderful creaminess, or Parmesan, which is more delicate in taste and provides a slight crunch. Grated sharp Cheddar is also tasty. SERVES 5–6 AS AN APPETIZER, 3–4 AS A MAIN COURSE

(18 MINUTES UNDER HIGH PRESSURE)

1 tablespoon unsalted butter
1 tablespoon olive oil
1 large onion, finely chopped
1 garlic clove, finely minced
1 celery stalk, finely minced
1 1/2 cups pearl barley, picked over and rinsed
1/3 cup loosely packed dried mushrooms (1/2 ounce)
4 cups chicken or vegetable broth or bouillon
2 1/4 cups water
2/3 to 1 cup crumbled blue cheese or 1 to 1 1/2 cups grated Parmesan
2 to 3 tablespoons minced fresh parsley (optional)
Salt (optional)

Heat the butter and oil in the cooker. Sauté the onion and garlic until the onion is soft but not browned, about 3 minutes. Stir in the celery and barley until the barley is coated with the fat. Add the mushrooms, broth, and water.

Lock the lid in place and over high heat bring to high pressure. Adjust the heat to maintain high pressure and cook for 18 minutes. Quick-release the pressure by setting the cooker under cold, running water. Remove the lid, tilting it away from you to allow steam to escape.

The risotto should be slightly soupy, but if there is more than about 1/3 cup of unabsorbed liquid, tip off the excess. While cooking over low heat, stir in the cheese and parsley (if desired). Add salt to taste (if desired) and serve immediately.

WHOLE GRAINS BEYOND BROWN RICE

The amount of time it takes for whole grains to cook and the amount of liquid they absorb varies according to the grain's age and the location of harvest and storage. To accommodate these variations, I recommend using an ample 4 cups of liquid per 1 cup of grain.

Pressure-cook the grains for the minimum time recommended; then, if more cooking is required, either return the cooker to high pressure or simmer the grains, covered, for a few more minutes. Drain off excess liquid before serving. For a fluffier final product, immediately return the drained grains to the pot and replace the lid, allowing them to steam in the residual heat for a few minutes.

For interesting variations, grains with approximately equal cooking times can be mixed and matched with each other, or with beans and legumes. Good combinations are wheat berries with chickpeas (page 251) and Job's Tears with anasazi or pinto beans (page 243).

Depending upon the menu, I often give the cooking liquid an aromatic lift by adding 3 or 4 quarter-sized slices of ginger and a bay leaf, or a few large cloves of garlic plus ½ to 1 teaspoon of dried herbs to the cooking liquid. Substitute vegetable, chicken, or beef broth or bouillon for all or part of the water, if desired. Any leftover cooking liquid can be stored in the refrigerator for up to 3 days and reused for grain cooking, with added water or broth. After repeated use, the cooking liquid becomes rather thick and can be used to give body to soups and stews. (Always sample the liquid first, as it may be slightly bitter or not to your taste.)

Some manufacturers discourage pressure-cooking grains for fear that the foaming action may catapult grains to the lid and clog the vent. By taking a few precautions, you should experience no difficulty whatsoever:

1. Always add 1 tablespoon of oil or butter per 1 cup of dry grain, and fill the cooker only to the halfway mark.

2. Quick-release pressure under cold running water.

3. In the unlikely event that you hear loud sputtering while cooking grains, or see water dripping down the sides of the pot, immediately take the cooker off the heat and place it under cold running water to bring the pressure down. When the lid is cool enough to handle, remove it and clean both the vent and the rubber gasket. Lock the lid back into place and proceed with cooking under pressure.

Basic Grains

I've developed two basic methods for cooking grains. One is boiled under pressure; the other is first toasted in oil to enhance the flavor and then boiled. Either method may be used with the grains listed in the chart.

Specific recipes for cooking millet, quinoa, and amaranth are given later in the chapter. I don't recommend pressure-cooking bulgur wheat or buckwheat groats (kasha), since they are relatively quick-cooking using standard methods and quickly turn to mush under pressure.

Here are some general guidelines:

- Use 1 tablespoon of oil or butter and 4 to 4½ cups of liquid for each cup of grain.
- Add 3 cups of water and 1 tablespoon of oil for each additional cup of grain.
- Don't fill the cooker beyond the halfway mark.
- When cooking time is up, allow the pressure to come down naturally, which is a calculated part of the cooking time. (Using a quick-release method causes the grains to burst open and lose their shape.) If the grains are not tender, replace (but do not lock) the lid and simmer until done.
- Once the grains are cooked to the desired consistency, drain well.

Basic Boiled Grains

1 cup grains

4^1/$_2$ cups water, vegetable, beef, or chicken broth or bouillon

1 tablespoon oil

^{1}/$_2$ teaspoon salt, or to taste (less if using canned broth or bouillon)

Seasoning of your choice, such as sliced fresh ginger, and/or halved
garlic cloves, and/or ^{1}/$_2$ teaspoon dried herbs, and/or 1 bay leaf

Pick over the grains, removing any gravel or discolored bits. Rinse and drain. Place the grains, liquid, oil, salt (if using), and seasonings in the cooker. Lock the lid in place and over high heat bring to high pressure. Adjust the heat to maintain high pressure and cook for the recommended amount of time (see preceding chart). Allow the pressure to come down naturally. Remove the lid, tilting it away from you to allow steam to escape.

If the grains are still very chewy, lock the lid back in place and return to high pressure for a few more minutes; if slightly underdone, replace the lid and cook over low heat for a few more minutes. When done, drain off any excess liquid and reserve it, if desired. For drier, fluffier grains, immediately return the cooked grains to the pot and replace the lid, allowing them to steam in the residual heat for a few minutes.

GRAIN COOKING TIMES AT A GLANCE

GRAIN (1 CUP)	CUPS LIQUID	OIL	OPTIONAL SALT	MINUTES UNDER HIGH PRESSURE, THEN NATURAL PRESSURE RELEASE	YIELD IN CUPS
WHOLE BARLEY	4$\frac{1}{2}$	2 T	$\frac{1}{2}$ T	25–27	3$\frac{1}{2}$
BARLEY (PEARL)	4$\frac{1}{2}$	2 T	$\frac{1}{2}$ T	18–20	3$\frac{1}{2}$
JOB'S TEARS	4$\frac{1}{2}$	1 T	$\frac{1}{2}$ T	15–17	2
OATS (WHOLE GROATS)	4	1 T	$\frac{1}{2}$ T	25–30	2
TRITICALE	4$\frac{1}{2}$	1 T	$\frac{1}{2}$ T	30–35	2
WHOLE RYE BERRIES	4$\frac{1}{2}$	1 T	$\frac{1}{2}$ T	25–30	2$\frac{1}{4}$
WHOLE WHEAT BERRIES	4$\frac{1}{2}$	1 T	$\frac{1}{2}$ T	35–40	2

Basic Toasted Grains

This is the preferred method if you like grains with the enhanced taste that results from toasting. Keep in mind, however, that toasting creates fissures in the bran layer, causing the grains to burst open and lose their shape.

1 cup grains

1 to 2 tablespoons oil

4 1/2 cups boiling water, vegetable, beef, or chicken broth, or bouillon

1/2 teaspoon salt, or to taste (less if using canned broth or bouillon)

Seasoning of your choice, such as sliced fresh ginger, and/or halved garlic cloves, and/or 1/2 teaspoon dried herbs, and/or 1 bay leaf

Pick over the grains, removing any gravel or discolored bits. Rinse and drain thoroughly. Place the grains in the cooker and cook over medium heat, stirring frequently, until the grains dry and begin to pop and emit a "toasty" aroma, 3 to 4 minutes. Stir in the oil until the grains are well coated. Add the boiling liquid (watch out for sputtering oil), optional salt, and seasoning.

Lock the lid in place and over high heat bring to high pressure. Adjust the heat to maintain high pressure, and cook for the recommended amount of time (see the chart on page 239). Allow the pressure to come down naturally. Remove the lid, tilting it away from you to allow steam to escape.

If the grains are not tender, return to high pressure for a few more minutes; if slightly underdone, replace the lid and cook over low heat for a few more minutes. When done, drain off any excess liquid and reserve it, if desired. For drier, fluffier grains, immediately return the cooked grains to the pot and replace the lid, allowing them to steam in the residual heat for a few minutes.

Grain Salad with Marinated Artichoke Hearts and Sun-dried Tomatoes

Try this colorful salad with cooked rice, pearl barley, Job's Tears, or quinoa. For a more intensely flavored dressing, include 1 to 2 tablespoons of the artichoke or sun-dried tomato marinating oil in place of an equivalent amount of olive oil.

SERVES 6

4 to 5 cups cooked grains, cooled to room temperature
1 cup coarsely chopped marinated artichoke hearts
1/4 cup finely minced sun-dried tomatoes, packed in oil
1/2 cup tightly packed, minced fresh basil, cilantro, or parsley
1/4 to 1/3 cup olive oil
Juice of 1 large lemon or lime (about 1/4 cup), or more to taste
Salt and freshly ground black pepper
Garnish: Greek olives (optional)

In a large bowl or storage container, combine the ingredients and toss to blend thoroughly. Adjust the seasonings. Let sit at room temperature for about 10 minutes before serving. Garnish with olives, if desired.

Grain Salad with Soy-Lime Vinaigrette

I highly recommend trying this salad with wheat berries (whole-grain wheat), which make an intriguing substitute for rice or pasta in most cold salad recipes. Keep in mind that wheat berries are denser and chewier than most cooked grains, so it's a good idea to surround them with "watery" ingredients like bell peppers and corn. If you're feeling ambitious, hollow out raw zucchini boats or tomato halves and heap the salad in them.

SERVES 6

4 cups cooked wheat berries, rice, or barley, cooled to room
    temperature
1 large red or green bell pepper, seeded and diced
2 cups cooked corn kernels or diced raw zucchini
$1/2$ cup tightly packed, minced cilantro
$3/4$ cup (approximately) Soy-Lime Vinaigrette (below) or other
    dressing

Set the cooked grains in a large bowl. Toss in the bell pepper, corn, and basil. Sprinkle on the dressing, adding enough to thoroughly coat the salad. Adjust the seasonings and serve.

Soy-Lime Vinaigrette

YIELD: APPROXIMATELY $3/4$ CUP

$1/3$ cup freshly squeezed lime juice
$1/4$ cup fruity olive oil
2 tablespoons soy sauce, preferably Japanese shoyu or tamari
2 teaspoons Dijon mustard

In a small jar, combine all of the ingredients. Shake vigorously until well blended. Refrigerate for up to 5 days.

Job's Tears Casserole

Job's Tears is an ancient Asian grain called hato mugi *in Japanese. They are available in Asian markets (usually mislabeled "barley") and some health-food stores. The fat white kernels look a bit more like beans than grains. They expand to about double their size in cooking, and have a slightly chewy texture that resembles pearl barley.*

Job's Tears are a good source of fiber and are high in vegetable protein and a number of essential minerals including iron, phosphorus, magnesium, and zinc. They have a mild taste reminiscent of corn and are worth seeking out.

In this casserole, I've combined Job's Tears with anasazi beans to create a complete protein. Anasazi (the Navajo word for "the ancient ones") have been used by Native Americans and Mexicans for centuries. They're a very tasty red-and-white bean with a slight sweetness. Feel free to substitute the more common pinto beans.

The casserole is soupy (although it thickens considerably on standing) and is best served in bowls, with a good whole-grain loaf for sopping up the sauce. SERVES 6

(15 MINUTES UNDER HIGH PRESSURE, THEN ABOUT 10 MINUTES FOR NATURAL PRESSURE RELEASE)

2 tablespoons olive oil

2 garlic cloves, minced

2 medium onions, coarsely chopped

3 celery stalks, thinly sliced

1 1/2 cups Job's Tears, rinsed and drained

3/4 cup dried anasazi or pinto beans, picked over and rinsed

4 1/2 cups water

1/4 pound large mushrooms, quartered

2 teaspoons dried oregano

2 bay leaves

2 tablespoons prepared mustard

Cayenne pepper or crushed red pepper flakes to taste (optional)

One 28-ounce can diced tomatoes, including juice
1 to 2 tablespoons soy sauce
1 to 2 teaspoons toasted (Asian) sesame oil

Heat the oil in the cooker. Sauté the garlic and onions, stirring frequently, until the onions are golden brown, 4 to 5 minutes. Stir in the celery, Job's Tears, and beans. Add the remaining ingredients except the tomatoes, soy sauce, and sesame oil. Stir well and scrape up any browned onions sticking to the bottom of the cooker. Pour the tomatoes on top. *Do not stir.*

Lock the lid in place and over high heat bring to high pressure. Adjust the heat to maintain high pressure and cook for 15 minutes. Let the pressure drop naturally, about 10 minutes. Remove the lid, tilting it away from you to allow steam to escape.

Stir in the soy sauce and sesame oil to taste. Check the Job's Tears and beans for doneness. If more cooking is required, cover (but do not lock) the cooker and simmer until done. Serve in bowls.

Basic Amaranth

This ancient Aztec grain has recently been rediscovered and is readily available in health-food stores. Amaranth is a better source of protein and calcium than most other cereal grains. It has the irresistible aroma of fresh corn.

The size and texture of uncooked amaranth is akin to crunchy poppy seeds, but it releases a starch while cooking, creating a silky sauce. Amaranth makes a superb breakfast cereal or vegetable side dish somewhat like grits.

Rinsing amaranth is tricky since the seeds are so tiny. I don't find rinsing necessary, but if you wish to do so, line your strainer with cheesecloth.

MAKES 2 CUPS

(6 MINUTES UNDER HIGH PRESSURE)

1 cup amaranth

2 cups water

1 tablespoon oil

1/2 teaspoon salt, or to taste

1 to 2 tablespoons unsalted butter (optional)

Combine the amaranth, water, oil, and salt in the cooker. Lock the lid in place and over high heat bring to high pressure. Adjust the heat to maintain high pressure and cook for 6 minutes. Quick-release the pressure by setting the cooker under cold running water. Remove the lid, tilting it away from you to allow steam to escape.

Stir well, adding butter if desired. If the mixture is too thin, boil gently while stirring constantly until thickened, about 30 seconds.

Millet Pilaf

I haven't had much luck with plain-cooked millet in the pressure cooker; I find that it becomes porridgey too easily. But it works well in this pilaf. Toasting the millet is part of the secret.

For a drier and fluffier pilaf, use less liquid (3½ cups) and cook for 14 minutes. For a moister pilaf with a texture resembling stuffing, use more liquid (4 cups) and cook for 20 minutes. Don't hesitate to use water if you have no broth on hand. SERVES 5–6

(14–20 MINUTES UNDER HIGH PRESSURE, THEN 10 MINUTES FOR NATURAL PRESSURE RELEASE)

1½ cups millet, picked over and rinsed

2 tablespoons unsalted butter or oil

1 celery stalk, julienned or coarsely grated

2 large carrots, julienned or coarsely grated

One 3-inch stick cinnamon, broken in two

¼ teaspoon ground coriander

½ cup currants or raisins

½ teaspoon salt (less if using canned broth or bouillon)

3¼ to 4 cups chicken or vegetable broth, or water

2 tablespoons toasted sesame or sunflower seeds
   (optional)

Set the millet in the cooker and over high heat toast it, stirring constantly until the millet begins to pop and some of the kernels turn light brown, 3 to 4 minutes. Add the butter, stirring until it melts and coats the millet. Stir in the celery, carrots, cinnamon sticks, coriander, currants, and salt. Stir in the liquid.

Lock the lid in place and over high heat bring to high pressure. Adjust the heat to maintain high pressure and cook for 14 minutes for a dry pilaf or 20 minutes for a moist one. Let the pressure drop naturally for 10 minutes before removing the lid. Remove the lid, tilting it away from you to allow steam to escape.

Remove the cinnamon sticks. Taste and adjust the seasonings. If the millet is not quite done, stir in a few tablespoons of water if the mixture seems dry, replace the lid, and simmer for a few more minutes. Stir in the sesame or sunflower seeds before serving, if desired.

Basic Quinoa

Quinoa is a delicious and crunchy Andean seed. It looks a bit like couscous when cooked and has a higher nutritional profile than wheat. In the pressure cooker, it is done to perfection when just brought up toward high pressure and then allowed to cook, covered, as the pressure drops naturally.

I like to cook quinoa with a rich vegetable, chicken, or beef broth when I use it as a rice substitute. When I plan to use it as the base for a cold salad, I cook it with water.　　　MAKES APPROXIMATELY 4½ CUPS

(2 MINUTES GOING UP TOWARD HIGH PRESSURE, THEN 10 MINUTES FOR NATURAL PRESSURE RELEASE)

2¼ cups vegetable, chicken, or beef broth or water
1½ cups quinoa, rinsed and drained
Salt to taste (less if using canned broth or bouillon)

Bring the broth or water up to a boil in the cooker. Stir in the quinoa and salt. Lock the lid in place and immediately set the timer for 2 minutes. Over high heat bring toward high pressure. Turn off the heat after 2 minutes; then let the pressure drop naturally for 10 minutes without removing the cover. Remove the lid, tilting it away from you to allow steam to escape.

If the quinoa is not quite done (it should be translucent and have no opaque white dot in the center), replace the lid and cook over medium heat for a few minutes longer, adding a few tablespoons of water if the mixture seems dry. When the quinoa is done, drain off any excess liquid. Adjust the seasonings and serve immediately.

Savory Mushroom-Quinoa Pilaf

An appealing variation on a traditional theme.   SERVES 4–6

(2 MINUTES GOING UP TOWARD HIGH PRESSURE, THEN 10 MINUTES
FOR NATURAL PRESSURE RELEASE)

2 tablespoons olive oil or butter
1 large onion, coarsely chopped
1 garlic clove, minced
1 green or red bell pepper, seeded and finely diced
2 celery stalks, finely chopped
1/2 pound mushrooms, sliced
Pinch of crushed red pepper flakes (optional)
1/2 teaspoon dried oregano or dried basil
2 1/4 cups vegetable or chicken broth or bouillon
1 tablespoon prepared mustard, preferably Dijon
Salt to taste (less if using canned broth or bouillon)
1 1/2 cups quinoa, rinsed and drained

Heat the oil in the cooker. Sauté the onion and garlic until the onion is lightly browned, about 4 minutes. Toss in the bell pepper, celery, mushrooms, crushed red pepper (if using), and oregano. Sauté an additional 3 minutes, stirring frequently. Add the broth, mustard, and salt to taste, and bring to a boil. Stir in the quinoa.

Lock the lid in place and immediately set the timer for 2 minutes. Over high heat bring toward high pressure. Turn off the heat after 2 minutes; then let the pressure drop naturally for 10 minutes. Remove the lid, tilting it away from you to allow steam to escape.

If the quinoa is not quite done (it should be translucent and have no opaque white dot in the center), replace the lid and cook over medium heat for a few minutes longer, stirring in a few tablespoons of water if the mixture seems dry. Adjust the seasonings and serve immediately.

Quinoa Tabbouleh

A sensational use of quinoa! And pretty as well.

SERVES 6–8

4 to 5 cups cooked quinoa, cooled to room temperature
2 celery stalks, finely minced
2 large carrots, grated or finely minced
4 scallions, finely minced
2 cups finely minced fresh parsley
1/2 cup chopped fresh mint
1/2 to 3/4 cup olive oil, preferably a fruity green, flavorful oil
1/3 to 1/2 cup freshly squeezed lemon juice (see Note)
1 tablespoon Dijon-style mustard
1/2 teaspoon salt, or to taste
Garnish: cherry or diced tomatoes (optional)

In a large bowl, combine the quinoa, celery, carrots, scallions, parsley, and mint. In a jar, or using a food processor or blender, combine 1/2 cup olive oil, 1/3 cup lemon juice, the mustard, and salt until well blended. Pour over the quinoa mixture and toss to thoroughly coat the grains. Taste and add more olive oil, lemon juice, or salt as needed. Serve immediately or refrigerate until needed. Before serving, garnish with tomatoes (if desired).

NOTE: This salad often needs to be zipped up with additional fresh lemon juice after overnight refrigeration.

Wheat Berry–Chickpea Stew
This vegetarian stew combines wheat berries and chickpeas to create complete protein. Even when thoroughly cooked, wheat berries are tenaciously chewy—which is just what I love about them.

This is a soupy stew, best served in bowls.   SERVES 6

(35 MINUTES UNDER HIGH PRESSURE, THEN NATURAL PRESSURE RELEASE)

2 tablespoons unsalted butter or oil
1 large onion, coarsely chopped
3 celery stalks, cut into 4 to 5 chunks
1 1/2 cups whole wheat berries, picked over and rinsed
6 cups vegetable, beef, or chicken broth or bouillon
1/2 pound parsnips (4 to 5 small), peeled and cut into 3 to 4 chunks
3/4 cup dried chickpeas, picked over and rinsed
1/3 cup loosely packed dried mushrooms (1/2 ounce)
2 bay leaves
2 teaspoons caraway seeds
1/2 teaspoon salt, or to taste (less if using canned broth or bouillon)
1/3 cup chopped fresh dill

Heat the butter in the cooker. Sauté the onion until soft, about 3 minutes. Stir in the celery and wheat berries. Add the broth (watch for sputtering oil), parsnips, chickpeas, mushrooms, bay leaves, and caraway seeds.

Lock the lid in place and over high heat bring to high pressure. Adjust the heat to maintain high pressure and cook for 35 minutes. Let the pressure drop naturally. Remove the lid, tilting it away from you to allow steam to escape. If the wheat berries or chickpeas are not quite cooked, lock the lid back into place and return to high pressure for a few more minutes.

Remove the bay leaves and stir in the dill. Adjust the seasonings, adding salt to taste.

Desserts

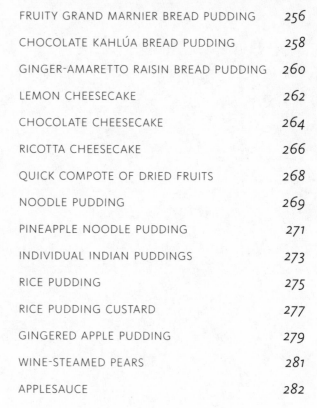

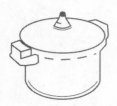

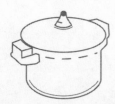

It may surprise you to find a dessert chapter in this cookbook, but there are some desserts that the pressure cooker does both quickly and remarkably well: compotes, custards, cheesecakes, and puddings—especially bread puddings. I had forgotten just how good some of these old-fashioned dishes could be until it became possible to create them on the spur of the moment.

BREAD PUDDINGS

Since bread puddings are not fussy, no hovering around the pot is required and worrying is absolutely forbidden: These dishes come out perfect every time. They're easy to create with stale bread and ingredients easily kept on hand; you'll feel inspired to create new combinations of liqueurs and fillings. My only caveat: If using a moist filling—such as sliced fresh fruit—reduce the amount of milk (or other liquid ingredients) accordingly.

To give them some shape, the puddings are cooked in a 5-cup soufflé dish, which fits conveniently into most 6-quart (and larger) pressure cookers. Before preparing a pudding, be sure to have an appropriate heatproof dish that can easily be lowered into the cooker and set on a trivet or steaming rack a few inches from the bottom. There should always be at least an inch of space between the pudding dish and the sides of the cooker.

Fruity Grand Marnier Bread Pudding

An elegant bread pudding studded with the rich flavor of dried fruit.

SERVES 6

(20 MINUTES UNDER HIGH PRESSURE, THEN 10 MINUTES FOR
NATURAL PRESSURE RELEASE)

2 to 3 tablespoons unsalted butter, plus butter for greasing the
    soufflé dish

7 to 8 1/2-inch-thick slices whole wheat or white Italian or French
    bread, left out 12 to 24 hours to dry

1 2/3 cups milk

1/3 cup Grand Marnier or other orange liqueur

4 large eggs, lightly beaten

1/4 cup honey

2 teaspoons grated orange zest

1/8 teaspoon freshly grated nutmeg

1 1/2 cups coarsely chopped mixed dried fruit, such as prunes,
    raisins, apricots, and dates

Garnish: ground cinnamon or 1/4 cup grated bittersweet chocolate

Generously butter a 5-cup soufflé dish or suitable alternative. Set
aside. Cut a piece of aluminum foil 2 feet long by 1 foot wide and double
it twice lengthwise to create a strip for moving the pudding dish to and
from the cooker. Set aside.

Butter the bread and cut each slice into 3 to 4 pieces. Arrange one-
third of the bread on the bottom of the soufflé dish.

In a food processor or with a whisk, combine the milk, Grand
Marnier, eggs, honey, orange zest, and nutmeg, and pour one-third of
this mixture over the bread, turning the bread pieces over so that they
can thoroughly absorb the liquid. Distribute one-third of the fruit on
top. Repeat layering bread, liquid, and fruit in this manner two more
times, or until the dish is about seven-eighths full.

Cover the dish with aluminum foil so that the foil fits tightly around the sides and tucks under the bottom but allows some room on top for the pudding to expand.

Set a trivet or steaming rack on the bottom of the cooker. Center the soufflé dish on the aluminum foil strip and carefully lower it into the cooker. Fold the ends of the strip over the top of the pudding. Pour in enough water to reach one-third up the sides of the pudding dish.

Lock the lid in place and over high heat bring to high pressure. Adjust the heat to maintain high pressure and cook for 20 minutes. Let the pressure drop naturally. Remove the lid, tilting it away from you to allow steam to escape.

Let the pudding cool for a minute or two before lifting the dish from the cooker with the aid of the foil strip. If you're not serving immediately, cut a few slits in the foil top and let it remain warm in the cooker, placing the lid ajar, for up to an hour. Before serving, dust the top lightly with the cinnamon or grated chocolate. To serve, scoop out the pudding with a large spoon.

Chocolate Kahlúa Bread Pudding *A must*
for chocolate lovers. This is a real winner. SERVES 6

(20 MINUTES UNDER HIGH PRESSURE, THEN 10 MINUTES FOR
NATURAL PRESSURE RELEASE)

2 to 3 tablespoons unsalted butter, plus butter for greasing the
    soufflé dish
12 to 14 1/2-inch-thick slices whole wheat or white, Italian or French
    bread, left out 12 to 24 hours to dry
1 2/3 cups milk
1/2 cup Kahlúa or other coffee-flavored liqueur
4 large eggs, lightly beaten
Two 3-ounce bars excellent-quality dark chocolate, coarsely
    chopped, preferably Lindt Excellence or Swiss Dark with Broken
    Hazelnuts

Generously butter a 5-cup soufflé dish or suitable alternative. Set aside.
Cut a piece of aluminum foil 2 feet long by 1 foot wide and double it
twice lengthwise to create a strip for moving the pudding dish to and
from the cooker. Set aside.

Butter the bread and cut each slice into 2 to 3 pieces. Arrange one-
third of the bread on the bottom of the soufflé dish.

In a food processor or with a whisk, combine the milk, Kahlúa, and
eggs, and pour one-third of this mixture over the bread, turning the
bread pieces over so that they thoroughly absorb the liquid. Distribute
one-third of the chocolate on top of the bread-milk mixture. Repeat
layering the bread, liquid, and chocolate in this manner two more
times, or until the dish is seven-eighths full. (Be sure to finish with a
chocolate layer.) Cover with aluminum foil so that the foil fits tightly
around the sides and tucks under the bottom but allows some room on
top for the pudding to expand.

Set a trivet or steaming rack on the bottom of the cooker. Center
the soufflé dish on the aluminum foil strip and carefully lower it into
the cooker. Fold the ends of the strip over the top of the pudding.

Pour in enough water to reach one-third up the sides of the pudding dish.

Lock the lid in place and over high heat bring to high pressure. Adjust the heat to maintain high pressure and cook for 20 minutes. Let the pressure drop naturally. Remove the lid, tilting it away from you to allow steam to escape.

Let the pudding cool slightly before lifting it from the cooker with the aid of the foil strip. If you are not serving the pudding immediately, cut open the foil top and let the pudding remain warm in the cooker, placing the lid ajar, for up to an hour. While the pudding is still warm, gently spread the top layer of chocolate with a knife to create a frosting. To serve, scoop out the pudding with a large spoon.

Ginger-Amaretto Raisin Bread Pudding

Raisin bread never tasted so good. SERVES 6

(20 MINUTES UNDER HIGH PRESSURE, THEN 10 MINUTES FOR
NATURAL PRESSURE RELEASE)

2 to 3 tablespoons unsalted butter, plus butter for greasing the
    pudding dish
7 to 8 slices raisin bread, left out 12 to 24 hours to dry
1²/₃ cups milk
4 large eggs, lightly beaten
¹/₂ cup Amaretto or other almond liqueur
1 teaspoon ground ginger
Pinch of salt
1¹/₄ cups dried apricots, coarsely chopped
Garnish: whole dried apricots

Generously butter a 5-cup soufflé dish or suitable alternative. Set aside.
Cut a piece of aluminum foil 2 feet long by 1 foot wide and double it
twice lengthwise to create a strip for moving the pudding dish to and
from the cooker. Set aside.

Butter the bread and cut each slice into 4 pieces. Arrange one-third
of the bread on the bottom of the soufflé dish.

In a food processor or with a whisk, combine the milk, eggs, Amaretto, ginger, and salt, and pour one-third of this mixture over the
bread, turning the bread pieces over so that they thoroughly absorb
the liquid. Distribute one-third of the chopped apricots on top of the
bread-milk mixture. Repeat layering the bread, liquid, and apricots in
this manner two more times, or until the dish is seven-eighths full.
Place the reserved whole apricots on the top of the pudding. Cover
with aluminum foil so that the foil fits tightly around the sides and
tucks under the bottom but allows some room on top for the pudding to
expand.

Set a trivet or steaming rack on the bottom of the cooker. Center the
soufflé dish on the aluminum foil strip and carefully lower it into the

cooker. Fold the ends of the strip over the top of the pudding. Pour in enough water to reach one-third up the sides of the pudding dish.

Lock the lid in place and over high heat bring to high pressure. Adjust the heat to maintain high pressure and cook for 20 minutes. Let the pressure drop naturally. Remove the lid, tilting it away from you to allow steam to escape.

Let the pudding cool slightly before lifting it from the cooker with the aid of the foil strip. If you are not serving the pudding immediately, cut a few slits in the foil top and let it remain warm in the cooker, placing the lid ajar, for up to 1 hour. To serve, scoop out the pudding with a large spoon.

CHEESECAKES

I think I made cheesecake twice in my life before owning a pressure cooker. It always seemed so delicate and fussy—not to mention the hours it took to prepare.

Would you believe a foolproof cheesecake in 30 minutes or less? With a velvety texture to boot. Eating is believing.

You'll need a 7- or 8-inch springform pan that fits comfortably into your pressure cooker with about an inch to spare between the pan and the sides of the cooker. Have the ingredients at room temperature before you begin. Avoid using reduced-fat cream cheese, which can prevent the cake from setting properly.

When you remove the aluminum foil cover after steaming, there may be a small puddle of water on the top of the cheesecake. This is not cause for concern: Just sop it up gently with a paper towel. The texture will not be affected.

These cheesecakes may seem small, but they are quite rich and can easily serve 8.

Store them in the refrigerator for up to 3 days and in the freezer for 3 months—they keep beautifully either way. Add toppings just before serving.

Lemon Cheesecake

This cheesecake, which is a snap to prepare, comes out slightly puffy, rather like a soufflé. I enjoy serving it warm in this form—a great boon when I haven't had the chance to prepare it ahead. If left to chill overnight in the refrigerator, it becomes firmer and denser, a typically creamy and rich New York–style cheesecake.

Drizzle some crème de cassis on each slice or serve the cheesecake whole, topped with sliced fresh strawberries or blueberries. It's also delicious without any adornments. SERVES 6–8

(15 MINUTES UNDER HIGH PRESSURE, THEN 7 MINUTES FOR NATURAL PRESSURE RELEASE)

Unsalted butter for greasing a 7-inch springform pan
1/3 cup granola
Two and a half 8-ounce packages Philadelphia cream cheese
    (20 ounces)
1 cup sugar
1 tablespoon grated lemon zest
2 tablespoons all-purpose flour
4 large eggs
1 large egg yolk
1/2 cup sour cream or plain yogurt
1 tablespoon lemon juice
1 teaspoon pure vanilla extract
Garnishes: sliced strawberries, blueberries, raspberries, or crème
    de cassis liqueur (optional)

Cut a piece of aluminum foil 2 feet long by 1 foot wide and double it twice lengthwise to create a strip for moving the pan to and from the cooker. Set aside.

Cover the exterior bottom and sides of a 7-inch springform pan with 1 large sheet of aluminum foil so that no water can seep in. Liberally butter the pan and distribute the granola, tilting and shaking to coat the bottom and the sides. Set aside.

In a food processor, blend the cream cheese, sugar, lemon zest, and flour until smooth, about 15 seconds. Add the eggs plus the yolk, the sour cream, lemon juice, and vanilla, and process for 5 seconds. Scrape down the bowl and process for another 5 seconds.

Pour into the prepared pan. Cover with buttered aluminum foil so that the foil fits tightly around the sides but allows some room on top for the cheesecake to expand.

Set a trivet or rack on the bottom of the cooker. Pour in $2^{1}/_{2}$ cups of water. Center the pan on the foil strip and gently lower it into the cooker. Loosely fold the ends of the foil strip over the top of the dish.

Lock the lid in place and over high heat bring to high pressure. Adjust the heat to maintain high pressure and cook for 15 minutes. Turn off the heat and let the pressure drop naturally for 7 minutes. Quick-release any remaining pressure. Remove the lid, tilting it away from you to allow steam to escape.

Let the cheesecake cool for a few minutes before removing it from the cooker with the aid of the foil strip. Set on a cooling rack, remove the foil, and let cool. If not serving the same day, refrigerate or freeze until needed.

Before serving, release and remove the sides of the springform pan. Serve from the base of the springform pan, garnished with strawberries, 4 blueberries, or crème de cassis, if desired.

Chocolate Cheesecake

The perfect dessert when you can't decide if you'd rather have cheesecake or chocolate mousse.

To prepare this recipe, first melt the chocolate and cool to room temperature. This version improves in taste and texture after overnight chilling. Top with plump, ripe strawberries for an elegant presentation and an irresistible flavor contrast.

SERVES 6–8

(20 MINUTES UNDER HIGH PRESSURE, THEN 10 MINUTES FOR NATURAL PRESSURE RELEASE)

Unsalted butter for greasing a 7-inch springform pan

1/4 cup chocolate cookie crumbs

Two 8-ounce packages Philadelphia cream cheese

1/2 cup sugar

2 tablespoons all-purpose flour

4 large eggs

1/4 cup sour cream or plain yogurt

Two 3-ounce bars excellent-quality dark chocolate, melted and cooled to room temperature, preferably Lindt Excellence or Surfin

Garnish: whole or sliced strawberries

Cut a piece of aluminum foil 2 feet long by 1 foot wide and double it twice lengthwise to create a strip for moving the pan to and from the cooker. Set aside.

Cover the exterior bottom and sides of a 7-inch springform pan with 1 large sheet of aluminum foil so that no water can seep in. Liberally butter the pan and distribute the cookie crumbs, tilting and shaking the pan to coat the bottom and sides. Set aside.

In a food processor, blend the cream cheese, sugar, and flour until smooth, about 15 seconds. Add the eggs, sour cream, and melted chocolate, and process for 5 seconds. Scrape down the bowl and process for another 5 seconds.

Pour into the prepared pan. Cover with buttered aluminum foil so that the foil fits tightly around the sides but allows some room on top for the cheesecake to expand.

Set a trivet or rack on the bottom of the cooker. Pour in 2¹/₂ cups of water. Center the pan on the foil strip and gently lower it into the cooker. Loosely fold the ends of the foil strip over the top of the dish.

Lock the lid in place and over high heat bring to high pressure. Adjust the heat to maintain high pressure and cook for 20 minutes. Turn off the heat and let the pressure drop naturally for 10 minutes. Remove the lid, tilting it away from you to allow steam to escape.

Let the cheesecake cool for a few minutes before removing it from the cooker with the aid of the foil strip. Set on a cooling rack, remove the foil, and let it cool to room temperature. Refrigerate overnight. Before serving, release and remove the sides of the springform pan. Serve from the base of the springform pan, garnished with strawberries.

Ricotta Cheesecake   *An Italianate and slightly lighter version of the New York–style cheesecake, this one is a real winner. Most of the raisins sink to the bottom, but no one seems to mind.*

Serve this light and delicious cake at room temperature, a few hours after you make it. It firms up and becomes somewhat denser with overnight chilling—an appealing alternative.

To appreciate the subtle lemony flavor, serve the cheesecake plain. For a more colorful version, garnish the top with raspberries or sliced fresh fruit, or a sprinkling of shaved chocolate or aniseeds.   SERVES 6–8

(25 MINUTES UNDER HIGH PRESSURE, THEN 10–15 MINUTES FOR NATURAL PRESSURE RELEASE)

Unsalted butter for greasing a 7-inch springform pan
1/3 cup granola
One 15-ounce container whole- or skim-milk ricotta
One 3-ounce package Philadelphia cream cheese
1 cup sugar
4 large eggs, lightly beaten
1/4 cup sour cream or plain yogurt
2 tablespoons all-purpose flour
1 tablespoon grated lemon zest
1/2 cup raisins, preferably golden
Garnish: raspberries or sliced fresh fruit, or a sprinkling of shaved
    chocolate or aniseeds (optional)

Cut a piece of aluminum foil 2 feet long by 1 foot wide and double it twice lengthwise to create a strip for lifting the hot pan from the cooker. Set aside.

Cover the exterior bottom and sides of a 7-inch springform pan with 1 large sheet of aluminum foil so that no water can seep in. Liberally butter the pan and distribute the granola, tilting and shaking the pan to coat the bottom and sides. Set aside.

In a food processor, blend the ricotta, cream cheese, and sugar until smooth, about 15 seconds. Add the eggs, sour cream, flour, and lemon zest, and process for 5 seconds. Scrape down the bowl and process for another 5 seconds. Stir in the raisins.

Pour into the prepared springform pan. Cover with buttered aluminum foil so that the foil fits tightly around the sides but allows some room on top for the cheesecake to expand.

Set a trivet or rack on the bottom of the cooker. Pour in 2½ cups of water. Center the pan on the foil strip and gently lower it into the cooker. Loosely fold the ends of the foil strip over the top of the dish.

Lock the lid in place and over high heat bring to high pressure. Adjust the heat to maintain high pressure and cook for 25 minutes. Turn off the heat and let the pressure drop naturally, 10 to 15 minutes. Remove the lid, tilting it away from you to allow steam to escape.

Let the cheesecake cool for a few minutes before removing it from the cooker with the aid of the foil strip. Set on a cooling rack, remove the foil, and let cool to room temperature. If not serving the same day, refrigerate or freeze until needed.

Before serving, release and remove the sides of the springform pan. Serve from the base of the springform pan; garnish, if desired.

Quick Compote of Dried Fruits   *Make a*

quick, simple, and elegant dessert (or gift) with foods from the pantry. This compote provides a wonderful way to put leftover wine and leathery dried fruit to good use.

Use any assortment of dried fruits except dates and apricots, which become mushy. Plump pear-shaped figs sold loose are better than those threaded onto a stick—the latter are tough-skinned.

Serve warm over ice cream or topped with whipped cream. It's quite rich, so a small portion goes a long way.   SERVES 4

(5 MINUTES UNDER HIGH PRESSURE)

3/4 cup red or white wine

1 1/4 cups water

3 slices lime or lemon

5 to 6 quarter-sized slices fresh ginger

One 3-inch stick cinnamon, broken in two

1/8 teaspoon ground cardamom

2 cups mixed dried fruits, excluding dates and apricots

Combine all the ingredients in the cooker. Lock the lid in place and over high heat bring to high pressure. Adjust the heat to maintain high pressure and cook for 5 minutes. Let the pressure drop naturally or use a quick-release method.

Remove the lid, tilting it away from you to allow steam to escape. Remove the cinnamon sticks and serve warm, or refrigerate in a tightly sealed container until needed (up to 2 weeks).

Noodle Pudding

Try drizzling some raspberry syrup or blackberry brandy over the warm pudding; the optional honey is for those who like their desserts very sweet. Pineapple Noodle Pudding, the recipe that follows, is a richer version.

SERVES 6

(15 MINUTES UNDER HIGH PRESSURE)

1 to 2 tablespoons unsalted butter, plus butter for greasing a 5-cup soufflé dish

3 cups loosely packed dry egg noodles (see Note)

$1/4$ cup raisins, preferably golden

1 large apple, cored, peeled, and grated

1 cup milk

2 large eggs

$1/4$ cup sour cream or plain yogurt (see Note)

$1/2$ teaspoon ground cinnamon

$1/4$ cup orange marmalade or apricot preserves

$1^1/2$ teaspoons lemon zest

1 to 2 tablespoons honey (optional)

1 tablespoon brown sugar

Garnish: additional ground cinnamon

Generously butter a 5-cup soufflé dish or suitable alternative. Set aside. Cut a piece of aluminum foil 2 feet long by 1 foot wide and double it twice lengthwise to create a strip for moving the pudding to and from the cooker. Set aside.

Cook the noodles in the pressure cooker (without the lid) for 5 minutes in rapidly boiling, salted water. Drain thoroughly and place in the prepared dish. While the noodles are still warm, add the butter and toss well to coat, then stir in the raisins and apple.

In a food processor or blender, combine the milk, eggs, sour cream, cinnamon, marmalade, lemon zest, and honey (if using). Stir this mixture into the noodles and sprinkle the top with brown sugar. Cover the soufflé dish with aluminum foil so that the foil fits tightly around the sides, leaving some room on top for the pudding to expand.

Set a trivet or steaming rack on the bottom of the cooker. Center the pudding dish on the foil strip and gently lower it into the cooker. Loosely fold the ends of the foil strip over the top of the pudding. Pour in enough water to reach one-third up the sides of the pudding dish.

Lock the lid in place and over high heat bring to high pressure. Adjust the heat to maintain high pressure and cook for 15 minutes. Let the pressure drop naturally or use a quick-release method. Remove the lid, tilting it away from you to allow steam to escape.

Let the pudding cool for a few minutes before removing it from the cooker with the aid of the foil strip. If you aren't serving the pudding immediately, cut a few slits in the foil top and let it remain warm in the cooker, placing the lid ajar, for up to 1 hour. Before serving, dust the pudding lightly with additional cinnamon. To serve, scoop out the pudding with a large spoon.

NOTE: You can substitute $3^1/_2$ cups leftover cooked noodles, but if they aren't slightly undercooked, the pudding's texture may seem too soft. If you use the yogurt, the pudding will have a very slight tang, and the honey should be added to counteract it.

Pineapple Noodle Pudding

A richer, moister pudding than the preceding one.

SERVES 6

(15 MINUTES UNDER HIGH PRESSURE)

2 tablespoons unsalted butter plus butter for greasing a 5-cup soufflé dish

2 1/2 cups loosely packed dry egg noodles (see Note)

1 cup sour cream or plain yogurt

1/2 teaspoon ground cinnamon

3 large eggs

2 tablespoons honey

1 1/4 cups crushed, canned pineapple in unsweetened pineapple juice (undrained)

1/3 cup raisins

1/2 cup coarsely chopped walnuts

1/2 cup granola

Generously butter a 5-cup soufflé dish or suitable alternative. Cut a piece of aluminum foil 2 feet long by 1 foot wide and double it twice lengthwise to create a strip for moving the pudding dish to and from the cooker. Set aside.

Cook the noodles in the pressure cooker (without the lid) for 5 minutes in rapidly boiling, salted water. Drain thoroughly and place in the prepared dish. While the noodles are still warm, add the butter and toss well to coat.

In a food processor or blender, combine the sour cream, cinnamon, eggs, and honey. Pour this mixture over the noodles, then add the pineapple, raisins, and walnuts. Stir well to distribute the ingredients evenly. Sprinkle the granola on top. Cover the soufflé dish with aluminum foil so that the foil fits tightly around the sides, leaving some room on top for the pudding to expand.

Set a trivet or steaming rack on the bottom of the cooker. Center the pudding dish on the foil strip and gently lower it into the cooker.

Loosely fold the ends of the foil strip over the top of the pudding. Pour in enough water to reach one-third up the sides of the pudding dish.

Lock the lid in place and over high heat bring to high pressure. Adjust the heat to maintain high pressure and cook for 15 minutes. Let the pressure drop naturally or use a quick-release method. Remove the lid, tilting it away from you to allow steam to escape.

Let the pudding cool for a few minutes before removing it from the cooker with the aid of the foil strip. If you are not serving the pudding immediately, cut a few slits in the foil top and let it remain warm in the cooker, placing the lid ajar, for up to 1 hour. To serve, scoop out the pudding with a large spoon.

NOTE: You can substitute $2^{1}/_{2}$ cups leftover cooked noodles, but if they aren't slightly undercooked, the pudding's texture may seem too soft.

Individual Indian Puddings

If you find the trio of molasses, ginger, and cinnamon as irresistible as I do, don't wait for Thanksgiving to prepare this treat. To make the puddings, you will need eight individual ½-cup ramekins. If the ramekins don't stack comfortably (pyramid fashion) in your cooker, cook in two batches. You can also halve this recipe to serve 4.

The cornmeal tends to settle to the bottom, creating a kind of two-tiered dessert with a light custard on top. Yummy.   SERVES 8

(8 MINUTES UNDER HIGH PRESSURE)

Butter for greasing 8 ramekins

2 cups milk

¹/₄ cup finely ground yellow cornmeal or quick-cooking polenta

Pinch of salt

4 large eggs, lightly beaten

1 teaspoon ground cinnamon

Generous ¹/₄ teaspoon freshly grated nutmeg

¹/₂ teaspoon ground ginger

¹/₄ cup molasses

¹/₄ cup loosely packed brown sugar

Generously butter the ramekins. Set aside. In a food processor, combine the remaining ingredients. Equally divide the liquid among the ramekins. Cover each with aluminum foil so that the foil fits tightly around the sides of each dish, but leaves some room on top for the puddings to expand.

Set a trivet or steaming rack on the bottom of the cooker. Pour in 2 cups of water. Set the puddings on the rack, building a pyramid as you go. Avoid leaning any dishes against the side of the cooker.

Lock the lid in place and over high heat bring to high pressure. Adjust the heat to maintain high pressure and cook for 8 minutes. Release the pressure with a quick-release method. Remove the lid, tilting it away from you to allow steam to escape.

Check for doneness by cutting a slit in the top of the foil. If the puddings are not set, lock the lid back in place and return to high pressure for an additional minute or two. Let the puddings cool slightly before removing them from the cooker. (Use tongs or wear an oven mitt.) If you are not serving the puddings immediately, cut a slit in each foil top and let the puddings remain warm in the cooker, placing the lid ajar, for up to 1 hour.

Rice Pudding

Best when still warm, this dry (as opposed to soupy) rice pudding is great right from the pot—comfort food at its very best! Plan to make it just before serving, if you can.

For a richer dessert, serve with a dollop of vanilla ice cream or sweetened whipped cream.

SERVES 6

(3 MINUTES UNDER HIGH PRESSURE, THEN 7 MINUTES FOR NATURAL PRESSURE RELEASE)

2 tablespoons unsalted butter

1 1/2 cups uncooked extra long-grain white rice

2 cups milk

2 cups water

1/2 cup raisins, preferably golden

Generous pinch of salt

1 teaspoon ground cinnamon

Generous 1/4 teaspoon ground ginger

1/4 teaspoon freshly grated nutmeg

1/3 to 1/2 cup firmly packed brown sugar

1 tablespoon molasses

1/4 cup heavy cream or half-and-half

1 teaspoon pure vanilla extract

1 teaspoon grated lemon zest

Heat the butter in the cooker. Stir in the rice, taking care that all of the grains are coated with the butter. Immediately stir in the milk, water, raisins, salt, and spices. Distribute 1/3 cup brown sugar and the molasses on top. *Do not stir.*

Lock the lid in place and over high heat bring to high pressure. Adjust the heat to maintain high pressure and cook for 3 minutes. Let the pressure drop naturally for 7 minutes. Quick-release any remaining pressure. Remove the lid, tilting it away from you to allow steam to escape.

If the rice is too chewy for your taste, replace the cover and let it continue to cook in the residual heat for another minute or two, stirring in a few tablespoons of warm water if the mixture seems quite dry. When done, stir in the heavy cream, vanilla, and lemon zest. Adjust the seasonings, adding extra brown sugar and spices to taste. Serve warm.

Rice Pudding Custard

A custardy rice pudding, richer and more traditional than the previous recipe. For an interesting change, substitute cooked brown rice for the white.   SERVES 6

(12 MINUTES UNDER HIGH PRESSURE, THEN 7–10 MINUTES FOR NATURAL PRESSURE RELEASE)

Unsalted butter for greasing a 5-cup soufflé dish
3 cups cooked rice
1/4 cup dried currants or 1/3 cup raisins
1 cup half-and-half or heavy cream
1/4 cup Grand Marnier or other orange-flavored liqueur
3 large eggs
1/3 cup firmly packed brown sugar
1 teaspoon pure vanilla extract
2 teaspoons grated orange zest
1/2 teaspoon ground ginger
1/4 teaspoon ground coriander (optional)
Pinch of salt

Cut a piece of aluminum foil 2 feet long by 1 foot wide and double it twice lengthwise to create a strip for moving the pudding dish to and from the cooker. Set aside.

Generously butter a 5-cup soufflé dish or suitable alternative. Add the rice and stir in the currants. In the bowl of a food processor, combine the remaining ingredients and process for 1 minute. Pour over the rice and lightly stir so that the liquid is well distributed. Cover the dish with aluminum foil so that the foil fits tightly around the sides, leaving some room on top for the custard to expand.

Set a trivet or steaming rack on the bottom of the cooker. Center the pudding dish on the foil strip and gently lower it into the cooker. Loosely fold the ends of the foil strip over the top of the pudding. Pour in enough water to reach one-third up the sides of the dish.

Lock the lid in place and over high heat bring to high pressure. Adjust the heat to maintain high pressure and cook for 12 minutes. Let the pressure drop naturally, 7 to 10 minutes. Remove the lid, tilting it away from you to allow steam to escape.

Let the custard cool slightly before removing it from the cooker with the aid of the foil strip. If you aren't serving the custard immediately, cut a few slits in the foil top and let it remain warm in the cooker, placing the lid ajar, for up to 1 hour. To serve, scoop out the custard with a large spoon.

Gingered Apple Pudding   *A soft custardlike pudding with a luscious flavor.*

SERVES 6

(15 MINUTES UNDER HIGH PRESSURE)

2 tablespoons unsalted butter at room temperature plus butter for
   greasing a 5-cup soufflé dish
1 cup coarse whole wheat bread crumbs, made from day-old bread
   (see Note)
1 pound apples, peeled, cored, and grated (about 3 cups)
1 cup milk
3 large eggs
2 tablespoons molasses
1/3 cup firmly packed brown sugar
1/4 cup sour cream
1/2 teaspoon ground ginger
1 teaspoon ground cinnamon
Pinch of salt
1/3 cup coarsely chopped walnuts (optional)
Garnishes: whipped cream and 2 to 3 tablespoons chopped, crystal-
   lized ginger (optional)

Generously butter a 5-cup soufflé dish or suitable alternative. Set aside.
Cut a piece of aluminum foil 2 feet long by 1 foot wide and double it
twice lengthwise to create a strip for moving the pudding to and from
the cooker. Set aside.

In a food processor, combine the softened butter and bread crumbs.
Transfer to a soufflé dish and stir in the grated apples. Set aside.

In the food processor, blend together the milk, eggs, molasses,
brown sugar, sour cream, ginger, cinnamon, and salt. Pour this liquid
and the walnuts (if using) over the bread crumbs and apples, and gently stir to blend. Cover the soufflé dish with aluminum foil so that the
foil fits tightly around the sides, leaving some room on top for the pudding to expand.

Set a trivet or steaming rack on the bottom of the cooker. Center the pudding on the foil strip and lower it into the cooker. Pour in enough water to reach one-third up the sides of the pudding dish.

Lock the lid in place and over high heat bring to high pressure. Adjust the heat to maintain high pressure and cook for 15 minutes. Let the pressure drop naturally or use the quick-release method. Remove the lid, tilting it away from you to allow steam to escape.

Let the pudding cool for a few minutes before removing it from the cooker with the aid of the foil strip. If not serving the pudding immediately, cut a few slits in the foil top and let it remain warm in the cooker, placing the lid ajar, for up to 1 hour.

Add the walnuts (if using) and garnish with whipped cream and ginger, if desired. To serve, scoop out the pudding with a large spoon.

NOTE: Crumbs should be slightly, but not bone dry. I like to use a hearty mixed-grain loaf, which makes delicious crumbs.

Wine-Steamed Pears

A quick-cooking treat for unexpected guests, the pears are infused with delicate flavor as they steam above spiced wine, which is then used as a thin sauce. They're best when served warm, but also good at room temperature. Sliced, they make a nice topping for pound cake or a genoise.

Work quickly once you've peeled the pears or they'll turn brown.

SERVES 4

(30 SECONDS–2 MINUTES UNDER HIGH PRESSURE)

1¼ cups dry white wine
½ cup cream sherry
¼ cup sugar
One 3-inch cinnamon stick, broken in two
½ teaspoon ground ginger
1 teaspoon grated orange zest
4 Bosc pears (ripe but firm), peeled

Combine the wine, sherry, sugar, cinnamon sticks, and ginger in the cooker. Bring to a boil and stir to blend. Simmer for 1 minute.

Carefully drop a steaming rack or basket into place. Trim the bottoms of the pears so that they will stand upright and set them on the rack.

Lock the lid in place and over high heat bring to high pressure. Adjust the heat to maintain high pressure and cook for 30 seconds. Reduce the pressure with a quick-release method. Remove the lid, tilting it away from you to allow steam to escape. If the pears are not sufficiently cooked, return to high pressure for another 30 to 90 seconds, as required. Reduce the pressure with a quick-release method.

Gently remove the pears with a slotted spoon and set on a serving platter or individual dessert plates. Remove the steaming rack and discard the cinnamon. If you wish, reduce the sauce by boiling vigorously until it thickens. Stir in the orange zest. Pour the sauce over the pears and serve warm or at room temperature.

Applesauce

The pressure cooker produces applesauce in a flash. For a more complex flavor, try a mixture of apples or half apples and half pears. To avoid peeling and coring the apples, simply pass the cooked sauce through a food mill or consider it a rustic applesauce and eat it, skins and all.

Stir in raisins or walnuts after the applesauce has cooked.

MAKES APPROXIMATELY 4½ CUPS

(0 MINUTES UNDER HIGH PRESSURE, THEN 5 MINUTES FOR
NATURAL PRESSURE RELEASE)

3 pounds apples, peeled, cored, and quartered

One 3-inch stick cinnamon, broken in two

2 crushed cardamom pods or ⅛ teaspoon ground cardamom
(optional)

1 cup apple cider or ⅓ cup applejack or Calvados diluted with
⅔ cup water

Grated zest of 1 lemon

Lemon juice to taste

Honey (optional)

Place the apples, cinnamon sticks, cardamom (if desired), and the liquid in the cooker. Lock the lid in place and over high heat bring to high pressure. As soon as high pressure is reached, immediately turn off the heat and allow the pressure to drop naturally. *Don't attempt to use a quick pressure-release method as the applesauce may sputter through the vent.*

Leave the applesauce chunky, or puree it with an immersion blender or in a food processor. Stir in the lemon zest, lemon juice, and honey (if desired) to taste.

NOTE: Since the apples release so much liquid, this recipe works in cookers that normally require more than 1 cup of liquid to come up to pressure.

Troubleshooting

On occasion the pressure cooker's behavior may puzzle you. Here are some explanations and potential solutions. If you continue to have difficulty, contact the customer service department for your cooker.

Always turn off the heat and release all pressure before attempting to check for any mechanical difficulties.

JT=jiggle-top or weighted valve cooker

SG=second generation spring valve cooker

The cooker is taking a long time to come up to pressure.

**You are cooking a larger quantity of food than usual. Be patient.

**There is insufficient liquid in the cooker.

**The cooker is filled beyond the recommended capacity and there isn't sufficient space for the steam pressure to gather.

**The lid isn't locked.

JT: The vent pipe is clogged with a particle of food. Quick-release any pressure under cold water, remove the lid, and clean the vent according to the manufacturer's instructions.

SG: The pressure regulator may be stuck. Tap the top of the regulator lightly with a spoon to release. If this doesn't help, quick-release the pressure and make sure the regulator is screwed in tightly.

Water is dripping down the sides of the cooker.

**The gasket isn't forming a tight seal. Try oiling it. If that doesn't work, purchase a new one.

Liquid or foam is spouting from the vent.

Immediately turn off the heat. Do not attempt to move the cooker until the pressure comes down naturally. Consider the following possibilities:

**The cooker is filled beyond capacity. Cook the ingredients in two batches.

**You are cooking foaming foods and have forgotten to add oil.

**Stir in a tablespoon of oil, clean the area around the pressure regulator, and resume cooking.

The lid won't come off even though all of the pressure has been released.

**A vacuum has been created inside the cooker. Either wait until the cooker cools entirely or bring it back up to pressure and quick-release. If the lid still does not come off, contact the manufacturer.

Food forms a crust or burns on the bottom of the cooker.

**Set a heat diffuser under the cooker while bringing up the pressure.

**Bring the ingredients to a boil before locking on the lid.

**Increase the liquid slightly the next time you cook the recipe.

Charts at a Glance

VEGETABLE COOKING TIMES AT A GLANCE
For Steaming Quick-Cooking Vegetables on a Rack Above Water
(See basic guidelines for steaming vegetables, page 170.)

APPROXIMATE MINUTES OF TOTAL COOKING TIME[†]

	0	1	2	3	4	5	6
ASPARAGUS							
* AVERAGE		•	•				
PENCIL		•					
BEANS, GREEN							
* WHOLE			•	•			
* HALVED OR FRENCHED			•	•			
BEET GREENS			•	•			
BROCCOLI							
* LARGE FLORETS			•	•			
* STALKS, PEELED, $1/4$-INCH SLICES				•	•		
* STALKS, PEELED, $1/8$-INCH SLICES			•	•			
BRUSSELS SPROUTS							
LARGE, 2 INCHES LONG					•	•	
* SMALL, $1^1/2$ INCHES LONG				•	•		
CABBAGE							
WHITE OR SAVOY, QUARTERED				•	•		
COARSELY SHREDDED		•					
CAULIFLOWER							
* LARGE FLORETS			•	•			
CELERIAC							
$1/2$-INCH DICE				•	•		
CELERY							
1-INCH SLICES				•	•		
CORN ON THE COB							
* LARGE, OLD				•	•		
YOUNG, FRESH			•	•			
EGGPLANT							
$1^1/2$-INCH CHUNKS			•	•			
LEEKS							
WHOLE, LARGE (WHITE PART ONLY)				•	•		
WHOLE, SMALL (WHITE PART ONLY)			•	•			
OKRA							
** SMALL PODS			•	•			
ZUCCHINI							
* $1^1/2$-INCH SLICES			•	•			

[†]The countdown begins the minute the lid is locked into place
*Steams effectively
**Flavor and texture improve with steaming
No stars: Steam only for purees

VEGETABLE COOKING TIMES AT A GLANCE

For Steaming Slower-Cooking Vegetables on a Rack Above Water (See basic guidelines for steaming vegetables, page 170.)

APPROXIMATE MINUTES UNDER HIGH PRESSURE†

	0	1	2	3	4	5	6	7	8	9	10	11	12	13	14	15	16	17	18	19	20	21	22
ARTICHOKES																							
* WHOLE, LARGE (9–10 OUNCES)												•											
* WHOLE, MEDIUM (6–8 OUNCES)									•	•	•												
* BABY (1 OUNCE EACH)				•	•		•	•															
BEETS																							
* WHOLE, LARGE (5–6 OUNCES)																					•	•	•
** WHOLE, SMALL (3–4 OUNCES)												•	•	•									
* 1/4-INCH SLICES				•	•	•																	
CARROTS																							
LARGE WHOLE							•	•	•														
** LARGE, 2-INCH CHUNKS					•	•																	
LARGE, 1/4-INCH SLICES		•																					
CHESTNUTS																							
* FRESH, UNSHELLED						•	•																
* DRIED, PEELED																•							
COLLARD GREENS																							
COARSELY CHOPPED						•	•																
KALE																							
COARSELY CHOPPED			•	•																			
ONIONS																							
* SMALL, WHITE (2 OUNCES)					•	•																	
SMALL, WHITE (1/2 OUNCE)			•	•																			

†The countdown begin the minute the lid is locked into place

	0	1	2	3	4	5	6	7	8	9	10	11	12	13	14	15	16	17	18	19	20	21	22
PARSNIPS																							
1-INCH CHUNKS			•	•	•																		
¹/₄-INCH SLICES		•																					
POTATOES, WHITE																							
MEDIUM (5–6 OUNCES), QUARTERED						•	•	•															
¹/₄-INCH SLICES			•	•																			
POTATOES, NEW RED																							
* WHOLE, MEDIUM (2 OUNCES)									•														
* WHOLE, SMALL (1 OUNCE)						•																	
POTATOES, SWEET																							
* LARGE (7–8 OUNCES), QUARTERED						•	•	•															
* ¹/₄-INCH SLICES			•	•																			
RUTABAGA																							
* ¹/₂-INCH DICE						•	•	•															
SQUASH																							
* ACORN, HALVED								•															
* BUTTERNUT, ¹/₂-INCH SLICES				•	•																		
* PATTYPAN, WHOLE (2 POUNDS)											•	•	•										
* WINTER, 1¹/₂-INCH CHUNKS				•	•																		
TURNIPS																							
* MEDIUM (4 OUNCES), QUARTERED				•	•																		
* SMALL (1¹/₂ OUNCES), WHOLE								•															
* ¹/₄-INCH SLICES		•	•																				

*Steams effectively
**Flavor and texture improve with steaming
No stars: Steam only for purees

BEAN COOKING TIMES AT A GLANCE

BEANS (1 CUP DRY)	MINUTES UNDER PRESSURE, THEN NATURAL PRESSURE RELEASE	YIELD IN CUPS
ADZUKI	16–21	2
ANASAZI	20–22	2¹/₄
BLACK (TURTLE)	22–25	2
BLACK-EYED (COW) PEAS	9–11	2¹/₄
CANNELLINI	28–32	2
CHICKPEAS (GARBANZO)	32–35	2¹/₂
CHRISTMAS LIMA	16–18	1³/₄
CRANBERRY	28–34	2¹/₄
FAVA*	22–28	2
FLAGEOLETS	28–34	2
GREAT NORTHERN	25–30	2¹/₄
LENTILS	2–4	2
LIMA (LARGE)**	9–10	2¹/₂
LIMA (BABY)	13–15	2¹/₂
NAVY (PEA)	22–25	2
PEAS (SPLIT, GREEN)	10–12	2
PEAS (WHOLE, GREEN)	16–18	2
PIGEON PEAS (GANDULES)	20–25	3
PINTO	22–25	2¹/₄
NAVY (PEA)	16–25	2
RED KIDNEY	25–30	2
SCARLET RUNNER	17–20	1¹/₂
SOYBEANS (BEIGE)**	28–35	2¹/₄
SOYBEANS (BLACK)**	32–37	2¹/₂

*Skins remain leathery after cooking and must be removed before serving unless the beans are pureed

**Require 2 tablespoons of oil for each cup of dried beans

WHITE RICE COOKING CHART

FOR A DRY RICE, USE THE SMALLER AMOUNT OF LIQUID. FOR A MOIST RICE, USE THE MAXIMUM.

EXTRA LONG-GRAIN WHITE RICE	CUPS LIQUID	OPTIONAL SALT	OIL/BUTTER	YIELD IN CUPS
1 CUP	$1^1/_2$–$1^3/_4$	$^1/_2$ T	1 T	3
$1^1/_2$ CUPS	$2^1/_4$–$2^1/_2$	$^3/_4$ T	1 T	4–$4^1/_2$
2 CUPS	3–$3^1/_4$	1 T	2 T	$5^1/_2$–6
3 CUPS	$4^1/_4$–$4^1/_2$	$1^1/_2$ T	$2^1/_2$ T	$7^1/_2$–8

Do not cook more than 3 cups of dry white rice in a 6-quart cooker.

BROWN RICE COOKING CHART

BROWN RICE	CUPS BOILING LIQUID	OPTIONAL SALT	OIL	APPROXIMATE YIELD IN CUPS
1 CUP	$1^3/_4$	$^1/_2$ T	1 T	$2^1/_4$
$1^1/_2$ CUPS	$2^1/_2$	$^3/_4$ T	1 T	$3^1/_2$
2 CUPS	$3^1/_2$	1 T	$1^1/_2$ T	5
3 CUPS	5	$1^1/_2$ T	2 T	7
4 CUPS	$6^1/_2$	2 T	2 T	10

Do not fill the cooker beyond the halfway mark. Cook under high pressure for 15 minutes. Let the pressure drop naturally for at least 10 minutes.

GRAIN COOKING TIMES AT A GLANCE

GRAIN (1 CUP)	CUPS LIQUID	OIL	OPTIONAL SALT	MINUTES UNDER HIGH PRESSURE, THEN NATURAL PRESSURE RELEASE	YIELD IN CUPS
WHOLE BARLEY	$4^1/_2$	2 T	$^1/_2$ T	25–27	$3^1/_2$
BARLEY (PEARL)	$4^1/_2$	2 T	$^1/_2$ T	18–20	$3^1/_2$
JOB'S TEARS	$4^1/_2$	1 T	$^1/_2$ T	15–17	2
OATS (WHOLE GROATS)	4	1 T	$^1/_2$ T	25–30	2
TRITICALE	$4^1/_2$	1 T	$^1/_2$ T	30–35	2
WHOLE RYE BERRIES	$4^1/_2$	1 T	$^1/_2$ T	25–30	$2^1/_4$
WHOLE WHEAT BERRIES	$4^1/_2$	1 T	$^1/_2$ T	35–40	2

Index

G

Garlic
  -Braised Brussels Sprouts, 134
  Gremolata, 91–92
Gaskets, rubber, 15, 284
Ginger-Amaretto Raisin Bread
    Pudding, 260–61
Gingered Apple Pudding, 279–80
Gingered Butternut Squash with
    Pineapple, 161
Grain(s). *See also* Rice
  Barley Risotto, 235
  Basic Amaranth, 245
  Basic Quinoa, 248
  Boiled, Basic, 238
  cooking times at a glance, 239
  exotic, buying, 215
  Individual Indian Puddings, 273–74
  Job's Tears Casserole, 243–44
  Lentil Soup with Prunes and
    Pears, 52
  Millet Pilaf, 246–47
  Mushroom-Barley Soup, 42–43
  pressure-cooking, notes about,
    236–37
  Quick Skillet-Fried Rice or Barley,
    223
  Quinoa Tabbouleh, 250
  Salad with Marinated Artichoke
    Hearts and Sun-dried Tomatoes,
    241
  Salad with Soy-Lime Vinaigrette,
    242
  Savory Mushroom-Quinoa Pilaf,
    249
  Scotch Broth, 37
  Toasted, Basic, 240
  Wheat Berry–Chickpea Stew, 251
Grand Marnier Bread Pudding, Fruity,
    256–57
Granola-Stuffed Acorn Squash,
    163–64
Green Beans
  Minestrone, 40–41
  pressure-steaming directions,
    174–75
  pressure-steaming times, 186
  with Tomatoes, 131

Greens. *See also* Cabbage
  Beet, and Sweet Potatoes, Beet Soup
    with, 48–49
  beet, pressure-steaming directions,
    180
  beet, pressure-steaming times,
    187
  Chicken with Lentils and Spinach,
    113–14
  collard, pressure-steaming direc-
    tions, 180
  collard, pressure-steaming times,
    188
  Collards with Bacon, 147
  kale, pressure-steaming directions,
    180
  kale, pressure-steaming times,
    188
  Kale and Potatoes, 151–52
Gremolata, 91–92
Gruyère
  Ham and Melted Cheese "Pudding,"
    106–7
  and Parmesan, Risotto with, 230
Gumbo, Chicken, 120–21

H

Ham
  An Unconventional Jambalaya,
    108–9
  Brunswick Stew, 122–23
  and Melted Cheese "Pudding,"
    106–7
  Quick Skillet-Fried Rice or Barley,
    223
High-altitude cooking, 14
Hoppin' John, 211

I

Indian Puddings, Individual,
    273–74

J

Jambalaya, An Unconventional,
    108–9
Job's Tears
  Casserole, 243–44
  cooking times, 239

K

Kahlúa Chocolate Bread Pudding, 258–59
Kale
  and Potatoes, 151–52
  pressure-steaming directions, 180
  pressure-steaming times, 188
Kasha, note about, 237
Kidney beans
  Beef Chili, 75–76
  cooking times, 196
  Refried Beans, 197
Kitchen timers, 16

L

Lamb
  Curry, 86–87
  with Olives, 85
  pressure-cooking, notes about, 81
  and Sausage, Pork and Bean
    Casserole with, 102–3
  Scotch Broth, 37
  Stew with Two Peppers, 82–83
  Tagine, Moroccan, 84
Leek(s)
  Braised, 153
  cleaning and chopping, 22
  Mushrooms, and Olives, Risotto
    with, 232
  and Potatoes, Cabbage with,
    136–37
  and Potato Soup, Creamy, 56
  pressure-steaming directions,
    180–81
  pressure-steaming times, 187
Legumes. See Bean(s); Lentil(s); Split
    Pea(s)
Lemon(s)
  Cheesecake, 262–63
  Gremolata, 91–92
  zesting, 22
Lentil(s)
  and Brown Rice Stew, 226
  cooking times, 196
  Side Dish, Quick, 209
  Soup, Quick, 209
  Soup with Prunes and Pears, 52
  and Spinach, Chicken with, 113–14

Lima Bean(s)
  Brunswick Stew, 122–23
  cooking times, 196
  –Vegetable Soup, 45
Lime(s)
  juicing, 23
  -Soy Vinaigrette, 242
  wedges, cutting, 23
  zesting, 22

M

Meat. See Beef; Lamb; Pork; Veal
Meatballs, Porcupine, 77–78
Mexican-Style Pork Stew, 98–99
Millet Pilaf, 246–47
Minestrone, 40–41
Miso-Chickpea Dressing, 203
Miso-Sesame Cabbage, 138–39
Moroccan Lamb Tagine, 84
Mozzarella, Smoked, and Sun-dried
    Tomatoes, Risotto with, 231
Mushroom(s)
  -Barley Soup, 42–43
  Chicken Cacciatore, 115–16
  Olives, and Leeks, Risotto with, 232
  Quick Skillet-Fried Rice or Barley, 223
  -Quinoa Pilaf, Savory, 249

N

Navy Bean(s)
  Boston "Baked" Beans, 206–7
  cooking times, 196
  Minestrone, 40–41
  Pork and Bean Casserole with
    Sausage and Lamb, 102–3
New England Fish Chowder, 36
Noodle Pudding, 269–70
Noodle Pudding, Pineapple, 271–72
Nuts
  Brown Rice with Chestnuts, Prunes,
    and Apricots, 224–25
  chestnuts, pressure-steaming
    directions, 179
  chestnuts, pressure-steaming times,
    188
  Pineapple Noodle Pudding, 271–72
  toasting, 23
Nutty Carrot Soup, 54